Hope for Hurting Parents
Support Group
Facilitator Guide

Tom and Dena Yohe

Hope for Hurting Parents
Support Group Facilitator Guide

Copyright © 2017 Tom and Dena Yohe

ISBN: 978-1-945975-62-2

Cover by Doni Keene, Keene Ideas Creative, www.keene-ideas.com

Published by EA Books Publishing a division of
Living Parables of Central Florida, Inc. a 501c3
EABooksPublishing.com

DEDICATION

We would like to dedicate this manual to the one who qualified us to write it, without whom it never would have been possible—our daughter, Renee.

It may seem strange that the person who put us in the position of needing this kind of help ourselves, is the one we're dedicating it to, but it's not strange to us at all. That's how God works, turning the wisdom of our culture upside down. He takes the bad and turns it into good. He takes the most embarrassing parts of our lives and creates something we can be proud of out of the ashes.

Renee, having you in our lives gave us the opportunity for greater personal growth than we would have had without you. As your parents, we came face to face with our failures and weaknesses, and today we are not the same. Our experience drove us to search for something we couldn't find and moved us to create something new from the void.

Our mess has become our message.

Our pain has become our passion.

Because of what we went through as your mom and dad, we wrote this Hope for Hurting Parents Support Group Facilitator Guide. Now, many other hurting parents will come together and find the same comfort we have received from God.

"Praise be to the God and Father of our Lord Jesus Christ, the Father of compassion and God of all comfort, who comforts us in all our troubles, so that we can comfort those in any trouble, with the same comfort we ourselves have received from God. For just as the sufferings of Christ flow over into our lives, so also through Christ our comfort overflows" (2 Corinthians 1: 3-5).

TABLE OF CONTENTS

THANK YOU

Thank you to the many parents who took the time to tell us how much help they received from our Hope for Hurting Parents support group. We're also grateful to those who wrote to tell us how much they wished they had a group like ours. God used them to prompt us to develop a tool to start more groups

We want to thank those who helped us bring this manual to reality. The following people have given their wisdom, skills, and time to edit our work: Gail Porter, Janet Richards, and Patti Ordower. Pam Findley got behind the vision to publish this Facilitator Guide and the accompanying Parent Notebook. She inspired others whose generously gave to help make it happen. Donni Keene did a wonderful job designing the cover. Thank you to each one of you for your efforts on this project.

Our deepest gratitude is to God who gave us the direction, wisdom, and perseverance needed to work hard until this was finished. He kept our focus on the encouragement, comfort, and hope we wanted these support groups to bring hurting parents.

MEET TOM AND DENA YOHE

Married thirty-nine years, Tom (M.Div.'79) and Dena have three children and two grandchildren. They served seventeen years in pastoral ministry and fourteen years with CRU (Campus Crusade for Christ), part of that time in Moscow, Russia.

Tom and Dena have a passion to help hurting parents because of their own painful ten year journey with their daughter Renee who has struggled with mental health issues, addiction, and self-injury. They have led support groups for parents like themselves since 2009. In 2011 they co-founded Hope for Hurting Parents, www.HopeforHurtingParents.com. Several years later they wrote this facilitator guide to help others start support groups.

Their mission is to give comfort, encouragement, and hope to hurting parents in their journey from surviving to thriving. This not only takes place in their support groups, but also in a variety of other ways: their website hosts a blog, a sign-up for encouraging emails, recommended books, websites, and resources. Personal meetings, phone calls, Skype appointments, intercessory prayer, social media, speaking and seminars are more ways they offer hope to brokenhearted parents.

In July of 2016, Dena published her book, *You Are Not Alone: Hope for Hurting Parents of Troubled Kids.* Together they have done interviews for TV and radio addressing their ministry and Dena's book. They have been featured on Family Talk with Dr. James Dobson, Family Life with Dennis Rainey and Bob Lepine, and Focus on the Family with Jim Daly and John Fuller.

The story of their daughter Renee's journey and her process of recovery is part of the worldwide movement called To Write Love on Her Arms (twloha.com). A movie was released by Sony in 2015 telling a fictionalized version of that story.

DENA'S BOOK

You Are Not Alone

*Hope For Hurting Parent's
of Troubled Kids*

In her book, Dena writes from experience and offers:

*Ideas to keep up your emotional and spiritual well-being when your world
feels as if it's crashing down.

*Suggestions for responding to friends who don't understand.

*Healthy ways to maintain other relationships and more.

*Includes prayers, exercises, websites, and other resources.

"Parents of prodigals often wrestle with feelings of profound loneliness and alienation. In
her moving account, Dena Yohe offers encouraging reminders that countless other
parents have been there too. Her wise and compassionate advice is sure to comfort and
uplift many hurting moms and dads."

Jim Daly, president of Focus on the Family

Available wherever fine books are sold.

3

MISSION STATEMENT

Our Mission: *To give comfort, encouragement, and hope to hurting parents on their journey from surviving to thriving.*

Our Support Groups exist to offer unconditional love and comfort to parents while providing them tools to gain strength and new perspectives.

- Experiencing Love and Comfort – you are not alone; you're safe
- Gaining Strength and Perspective – living each day with the big picture in view
- Building Courage and Hope – if things don't resolve, God is still there
- We do this because: parents often feel discouraged, hopeless, and isolated when dealing with a child/children who have gone "prodigal" from the family.

Our Passion: *A Hope for Hurting Parents support group in every community.*

We want to reach any parent inside or outside the church walls who is dealing with a child*:

- Who is abusing or addicted to drugs or alcohol (or any other addiction).
- Who has repeat offenses with the court and/or authority problems with the school system or is incarcerated.
- Who brings physical harm to themselves such as self-injury (cutting), suicide attempts or an eating disorder.
- Who defies parental boundaries by running away.
- Who engages in sexual behaviors, pornography, or has gender identity issues.
- Who has a mental illness and isn't coping well, making destructive decisions.

*This child can be any age, teen or adult.

INTRODUCTION

When we were going through our own painful parenting journey we didn't know where to turn for help. Since our daughter was dealing with alcohol and drug abuse we decided to attend Al-Anon meetings. We found them valuable and helpful, although most group participants were there for a troubled spouse.

Because our daughter had also been raped, we felt the need for more. After searching further, we found a hospital-sponsored support group for parents coping specifically with this issue. We faithfully attended it every week for a full year. It too, was beneficial.

Yet, something was missing. We longed to be part of a group just for parents that covered a broad range of issues, while also allowing for our Christian perspective. We wanted to include two elements that brought us our greatest comfort: the Scriptures and prayer.

We began to discuss what we might do and decided that when we felt more stable ourselves, we would start a support group, incorporating the best elements we'd experienced, adding the missing elements important to us. This is where Hope for Hurting Parents began.

A core belief is that we were not created to live life in isolation, but in community. Life with all its joys and sorrows is to be experienced with others. Mutual encouragement and shared trials helps to lighten our load and increase our strength for the journey. This is where the power of support groups can help when the pain is too deep to be alone.

In the spring of 2009 we held our first support group meeting in our home. We've continued to meet twice a month year round ever since, taking a week off in November and December for the holidays.

Over the years, we began to hear from hurting parents who lived in other parts of the country. They expressed the longing for a group like ours in their town. Our hearts ached to think of them suffering alone, in isolation. What could we do to help?

Many weren't ready to start a group or didn't know where to begin, even if they were. While we couldn't solve the issue of feeling ready, we realized we could do something about the other issue. Hence, the idea of writing a facilitator guide was born and we began the process in the spring of 2013. Our intention is to offer some structure and content for anyone who has the desire to reach out to other parents in pain.

As you will notice we've taken the emphasis off "leading" and placed it on "facilitating". Your role is not as a teacher or instructor; rather, you're simply a facilitator who shares content, asks a few open-ended questions, and guides discussion. You aren't expected to know everything or have your act together. We're all fellow strugglers on the same heartbreaking path. Authenticity and a willingness to be vulnerable with your trials, is your best asset.

We recognize that what we do and how we do it—the frequency our group meets, where we meet, and what we do—may not fit every situation. Feel free to structure your group as you see best. Our passion is for more Hope for Hurting Parent support groups to get started all over the country. There are many in need, with few resources. Please use this material any way you like.

The topics we've included can be used in any order you choose. Not all of them will hit home for everyone in the group. Perhaps principles will be gained that can help them in other relationships. On these occasions those parents can be a support to other parents in the group.

We consider your feedback, input, recommendations or suggested changes as important and invaluable. We welcome your comments: hope@HopeForHurtingParents.com

A FINAL WORD: It's not our intention to create groups that are strongly content driven. More than anything, our prayer is that the group you start will be a safe, confidential, loving community for hurting parents to find the encouragement, comfort, hope, resources, and acceptance they need. Therefore, do not feel like you have to get through all the material every time you meet. Feel free to skip over sections or stop short if you run out of time. Just be sure you've touched on the most important points in the session.

The goal is to give parents the opportunity to open up about their feelings with others who understand, won't think less of them or give pat answers. Once in awhile, you may have a distressed mom or dad who needs to talk and weep over their child. In those situations, we encourage you to cast aside your agenda and focus on that person. Let them talk it out and spend time praying for them as a group. These can be special times for everyone. Be flexible, ready to set aside your plans, if needed.

LET US KNOW HOW WE CAN HELP YOU.

Email questions to: hope@HopeForHurtingParents.com

PLEASE REGISTER YOUR GROUP!

Advantages:

1. Our team can come alongside you to offer ongoing support.

2. If you decide to have an open group, we can list it on our website to help others in your area find you.

Go to our website **www.HopeForHurtingParents.com/want-to-start-a-support-group/** and click on the button, **Register Your Group**.

BEFORE STARTING YOUR GROUP

Make the following decisions:

1. Decide when, where, and how often you will meet: weekly, bi-weekly, monthly. For example, we meet the 2nd and 4th Tuesdays of every month, from 7:00 p.m. to 8:30 p.m. in our home. Meet in a home if possible. It's the most comfortable environment and best for confidentiality. Meeting in a church is fine, too. There are pros and cons for each. You may want to try both and get feedback from the group.

2. Decide if your group will be open to people in the community or other churches. Make this known to the group each time you meet.

3. Decide if you want to offer a contact list. A notepad or sheet of paper is passed around at the beginning of each meeting following the guidelines. Group participants share their name and contact information for the purpose of connecting with each other between meetings. Parents can take a picture of the list with their cell phone. This is a great way to expand their support system.

4. Decide if you will offer a lending library. You can offer a wide variety of books for parents to check out. Provide a sign-out sheet to record books they borrow. Your church or other interested persons may want to help purchase these books.

5. Decide if you want to offer information on resources in your community.

   - You can gradually collect these over time

   - Names and business cards of counselors, psychiatrists, etc.

   - Other support and recovery groups like Al-Anon, Nar-Anon, Celebrate Recovery, AA (Alcoholics Anonymous), NA (Narcotics Anonymous), NAMI (The National Alliance on Mental Illness), etc.

   - Treatment Centers or Rehab Programs

6. Decide if you will offer refreshments.

   - Keep it light and simple; people don't eat much at this kind of group. We offer water, coffee, and tea; pretzels, nuts or cookies.

   - You could have a sign-up sheet for people to take turns bringing a snack.

7. If you meet in your home, you may want to put a "Come in!" sign on the front door. This will prevent being interrupted by a ringing doorbell when you have late-comers.

PRACTICAL TIPS

GUIDING DISCUSSION

1. Use open-ended questions:

   - "What do you think?"

   - "Tell me more about that."

   - "What comes to your mind when you read/hear that?"

   - "How does that make you feel?"

   - "What does someone else think?"

   - "Do you agree? Why or why not?"

2. Learn to be comfortable with silence:

   - Sometimes people need time to think before responding.

   - Resist the urge to talk too much, to give an answer.

   - Wait patiently for comments.

   - You may need to reword the question.

   - If the group seems reluctant to talk, direct them to turn to the person on their left or right and discuss the content. This is also an effective technique to change things up and do them differently sometimes.

HANDLING THE TALKATIVE INDIVIDUAL

Politely interrupt and say one of these:

   - "Thank you for sharing, now let's hear from someone else."

   - "I appreciate your input, let's give someone else a chance to share what they think."

   - "I really appreciate your participation, but let's continue this discussion after the group, when we have more time. Would that be alright with you?"

   - "Thank you for being so involved, who else wants to share?"

GUEST SPEAKERS

We've found parents enjoy it when guest speakers come to share with the group from time to time. It always draws a larger crowd and visitors.

Counselors, former prodigals who have overcome an issue, parents who have learned to live in peace and victory—their situation may not have resolved yet—are a few suggestions.

A counselor can speak on a topic or an area of expertise. We've had counselors speak on the following topics:

Grief and loss

Self-Care

Addiction

Adoption challenges

Coping with life's hurts

A counselor who was a former prodigal shared their story and their mother also came and shared insights.

Marijuana—questions and answers from a counselor who was an addictions specialist.

Mental Illness—insights from a counselor who specializes in this area who is also the parent of adult children living with mental illness.

Maintaining joy

A former lesbian shared how God brought her out of the lifestyle and into a ministry to help others overcome same-sex attraction.

Suicide prevention—a counselor held a workshop for us; we opened it up to the general public, advertised locally, and held it at our church.

PTSD—Post Traumatic Stress Disorder

EMDR—Eye Movement Desensitization Reprocessing

GROUP GUIDELINES

These guidelines are in the Parent Notebook. Have the group take turns reading each item on the list. Do this every time you meet.

Read, Disclaimer – We are not professional counselors, advisors or experts. We are parents, just like you, going through a painful experience.

1. This group is not a Bible Study but we refer to scripture; it's not a prayer meeting but we will pray for you and your children. It's not a place to find out how to fix your child, but what you learn may aid their growth.

2. This group is for you, the parent. You are the focus. It's a place for you to process feelings, talk about the struggles you're having with your child, grow personally and be encouraged by others who share similar pain.

3. This group is a confidential and safe place. What's said here stays here and who you meet here stays here. However, you are welcome to share the content and principles you learn here. If you see someone from the group in a public setting, be careful to not make comments about their child's situation that could embarrass them or compromise their privacy.

4. This group is a judgment free zone. We offer unconditional acceptance to one another. We are not here to compare each other's situations or invalidate each other's pain by minimizing what they may be going through.

5. Our goal is to be the best listeners we can be. Please don't interrupt each other or offer **unsolicited** advice. If asked, you are welcome to offer your ideas or insights, otherwise talk with the person after the group.

6. You never need to share or talk in this group. Participate only as you desire. But please be time conscious when sharing, so everyone will have the opportunity to talk.

7. All the content you hear may not always apply to you. We encourage you to take what you like and leave the rest.

8. Contact List: Each time we meet we'll pass around a sheet of paper for you to write down your name, phone number and/or email, so you can develop connections with each other and support one another outside the group time. Be sure to take some names and numbers with you, or simply take a picture of the list with your phone!

SAMPLE TIMELINE
(ADAPT THIS TO YOUR PREFERENCES)

7:00 - 7:15	Gathering - name tags, refreshments, socialize
7:15 - 7:35	Welcome, group guidelines, icebreaker, updates
7:35 - 8:10	Content and discussion
8:10 - 8:15	Bathroom break, refreshments
8:15 - 8:20	Prayer – divide up into small groups to pray (all men together most of the time and women into groups of 2-3) or stay together in the larger group.
8:30	Dismiss - say goodbye to those who need to leave. Others are welcome to stay longer. Adapt time after dismissal to facilitator's or host's needs.

1. Welcome, Guidelines, etc.

   - Open each session: have people take turns reading the Group Guidelines.

   - New Comers: to make new people feel welcome have returning parents say their first name and what their situation is (My name is_____, I am here because my ___ year-old daughter has problems with _____.) Then ask new people to share if they are comfortable. No pressure to talk. Watch the time closely here.

   - Group sharing: climate check

     • Ask how they are doing - if someone is in a crisis or has a significant need, the whole time may be spent allowing them to talk and then offering comfort, support and prayer.

     • Updates on their child (optional – first timers may be reluctant or too emotional); keep this very brief. This can tend to go long so we don't always include it, unless there is something very important someone wants to share.

     • Ice Breaker: a general non-threatening time to encourage people to begin opening up. Example: "On a scale of one to ten—one being not well at all and ten that you are doing really well—how are you doing tonight and why?" Or "Where are you in your grieving process?" The question may tie-in with your content. More examples are included in this guide.

2. Content and Discussion

   - Topic: introduce the topic for the session.

   - Discuss and interact on the topic. Be careful not to do all the talking. Ask good questions to encourage group discussion. Don't read everything yourself. Get the group involved by asking volunteers to take turns reading material.

3. Prayer

    - Suggestions: we like to be sure each child is prayed for by name.

- As a group together, if not too large. One idea is to form a circle, hold hands, and say something like this: "Let's envision each of our children in the middle of this circle as we surround them with love, praying for them and for ourselves."

- Break into smaller groups - keep men and women separate

- Groups of two or three - more time to share and pray

- One-on-one

- If you divide into smaller groups you can come back together for to close the meeting or tell them they are free to leave when they're finished praying. We make sure we dismiss the group at the appointed time. It's important to end on time.

*Experiment and choose what you like best or vary it each time you meet.

ICE BREAKER QUESTIONS

It is very effective if you can tie-in the ice breaker question with the topic of the content for your group session, but it isn't necessary.

- ❖ On a scale of 1 to 10 how are you doing today and why? (1 being not good at all and 10 being very good.)

- ❖ What were your worst and best moments since we met last? It doesn't have to be related to your child.

- ❖ On a scale of 1 to 10 rate your anxiety level and explain. (1 is low – 10 is high)

- ❖ Where are you in your grief journey? (shock, denial, sadness, angry, bargaining and acceptance)

- ❖ What adjective best describes how you feel about your child today?

- ❖ What is something that makes you unique?

- ❖ Share something you are thankful for today. It doesn't have to be related to your child.

- ❖ Share a favorite memory you have of your child.

- ❖ What color or word best describes your main emotion about your child today? Why?

- ❖ What would be your dream vacation if money was not a factor and why?

- ❖ What is a good thing that is happening in your life right now?

- ❖ How are you feeling about the coming holiday season and why?

- ❖ Where would you like to go for a one week vacation and why?

- ❖ What is one of your favorite holiday traditions? (Christmas, Thanksgiving, Easter)

- ❖ What makes you angry about your child's situation or your relationship with them?

- ❖ Think back as far as you can and draw a line graph to represent your life. (Hand out paper for this.) Consider the high points, the low points, moments of inspiration, moments of despair, leveling off times, and where you are now. The line will probably be a mixture of straight, slanted, jagged and curved lines. Give about 5 minutes then show them to the group all at once. Take time to look at them. Say something about one part of the graph. They'll see we all have our ups and downs.

- If your house was on fire, and everyone was safe what three or four objects would you save and why?

- What do you need most today on your parenting journey? (peace, strength, wisdom, etc.)

- How is your heart today and why?

- If you could go anywhere in the world, where would you go and why?

- Are you are an enabling parent? Why or why not?

- What did you do this past week to improve your well-being, for your self-care? What do you want to do?

- What are you doing that's helping you cope?

- You've been exiled to a deserted island for a year with none of your personal belongings. What would you miss the most and why?

- What do you like to do to relax?

- What's the hardest thing you've ever done?

- What was the best thing that happened to you last week?

- How have you been soothing yourself lately?

- If you could live last week over again, what would you do differently?

- What is one of your hobbies or favorite ways to have fun?

- In what ways are you distracting yourself or escaping the heartache you feel over your child? Is it working?

- Are you finding the comfort or help you need? Where?

- If you could change one thing about yourself what would you change?

- What would you like the group to know about you right now?

- If you could have any question answered, what would it be?

- What has been the biggest surprise for you on this journey?

- What hurts you the most about the situation with your child?

- How much hope do you have for your child today: high, medium, low or none? Why?

❖ Use only your hands to show your current attitude toward your child: praying hands, a fist, pointing finger, open hands with palms up, cover your face, hands on chest/heart, hands out and up as in asking a question or giving up, etc.

❖ If you could ask God any question and get His answer right now, what would it be? Write it down on index card, shuffle them, pass them out, each one reads one. No comments.

PRAYER STRATEGIES

Prayer is our greatest resource for peace, courage, and strength. Through our prayers God can do amazing things in our lives and in our children.

Here are a few suggestions for your prayer time:

1. Pray the Scriptures – look for promises (there are over 7,000 in the Bible) and make them into your prayers.

2. You can choose from many different ways:

   - Small groups (men and women separately).

   - Get into groups of two or three—men with men, women with women. We found groups of two works best for our time frame.

   - Stay together as a group and the facilitator prays, or invites participants to pray out loud for each other as they choose.

   - Stay together as a group and the facilitator guides participants to pray silently for the person to their left or right. The facilitator says, "Amen" at the end of the allotted time.

   - Stay together as a group but use a prayer included in the participant notes (or from another source) to pray in unison. (The Serenity Prayer, The Lord's Prayer, etc.)

   - Be creative.

Do whatever seems best to you. Take into consideration the people in your group, the environment you're meeting in, and the timeframe.

Books to help you pray:

These books are filled with prayers. You may want to purchase a few to use for this purpose. They are listed in the Appendix in the back of this guide in the Recommended Books and Resources section, along with more information on the two websites listed. They're also in the back of the Parent Notebook.

Hope of a Homecoming by Brendan O'Rourke and DeEtte Sauer

How to Pray for Lost Loved Ones by Dutch Sheets

Moments for Families with Prodigals; most recent edition is called: *Prayers and Promises for Worried Parents* by Robert J. Morgan

Praying for Addicted Loved Ones: 90 in 90 by Sharron Cosby

Praying God's Will for My Daughter by Lee Roberts

Praying God's Will for My Son by Lee Roberts

Praying for Your Prodigal Daughter by Janet Thompson

Praying Prodigals Home by Sherrer and Garlock

Praying the Scriptures for Your Teenagers by Jodie Bernt

Praying Your Prodigal Home by Richard Burr

Prayers for Prodigals: 90 Days of Prayer for Your Child by James Banks

Reclaiming Surrendered Ground by Jim Logan

The Power of A Praying Parent and Praying for Your Adult Child by Stormie Omartian

Websites:

Prayer for Prodigals – www.prayerforprodigals.com

Breakthrough – www.intercessors.org

WHAT OTHERS ARE SAYING

Parents

> "I really needed this tonight. Being with others who understand and don't judge me is so freeing. My heart feels so much lighter. I really needed the topic of detachment, too. I have a lot to work on, but now I feel like I can do it!"

> "About 4 years ago, I felt very alone with my situation experiencing much chaos in my life with my son living in the house addicted to drugs and alcohol. I felt like I was beginning to slip into a pattern of internalizing everything that was happening feeling very angry, sad, depressed and hopeless that things would never change. I decided I would try a group and keep an open mind. If it didn't work or it was too awkward, I wouldn't go again."

It was so helpful I decided I would keep going as much as I could and looked forward to the next meeting. The topics were relevant and interactive. It was very healing to discuss my situation and feelings. I liked hearing from other moms who were experiencing pain with their teens or adult children."

> "I really appreciated the topic in print. I had something tangible I could hang on to and look at again and again during times of crisis, offering scripture and hope. Most of all, the group supported me with their prayers, which helped me to regain my focus on God's strength instead of my own. I now realize that my son's situation is not hopeless."

> "We cannot thank you enough for your ministry. Over the past year, as we worked through the various stages of facing our son's choices, you have been there alongside us. Your ministry and group have been a real safe haven for us to catch our breaths."

> "Opening your home and offering warm hospitality, non-judgmental input, real-life empathy and shoulders to cry on, has been a real blessing for us (and I do not throw that word around lightly). And we know this is true for the many others who have stepped across your threshold. Your transparency with your own personal story has been courageous and humbling. You have encouraged us in numerous ways and we feel a strong bond of suffering with you both that we don't (can't) share with anyone else in our lives."

> "It was such a pleasure to be in the group. It is very comforting to know you're not alone. I was encouraged and found the handout helpful. I am thankful to be in a group where people share openly, and don't feel judged. It's been a long road, and I'm so encouraged after the meeting yesterday. I am truly glad and feel so much more at peace knowing that I have a safe place with others who share the same types of struggles."

Group Facilitators

> "Thank you for your ministry. Our group is going well. The Facilitator's Guide is a God send. Please continue this work."

> "The content is very rich and filled with wisdom. We have all felt that the material is very insightful and useful for us in our journey. There are many times we have shared how 'right

on' the material is in helping us navigate this uncharted territory."

➤ "The topics are so relevant in your material. I think every parent experiencing these types of situations can relate to them at some point in their journey with an adult child.
Leading a Hope for Hurting Parents group is very meaningful to me. God keeps leading me to others who are hurting. God used my situation to give me more compassion and encourage others in similar situations."

One woman in my group commented, 'Everyone needs a group like Hope for Hurting Parents.' She is right. I have talked to women in other states who have never heard about it and are interested in having one. There is a need for groups like these to love, support, pray for, and encourage one another through our struggles."

Church and Ministry Leaders

➤ "A Hope for Hurting Parents group provides immeasurable support, guidance, hope, and care to those who attend. I have watched and witnessed the profound affect this group provides to the hurting parents of our church community."
Berry Johnston - Pastor of C.A.R.E. Ministries, Discovery Church, Orlando, FL

➤ "I have had the privilege of getting to know Tom and Dena Yohe and their ministry, Hope for Hurting Parents. The Yohes have a tremendous testimony and are faithful witnesses to the healing power of Christ. We at New Covenant United Methodist Church have two Hope for Hurting Parents groups now. We seek their wise counsel and advice as we move through this process. I cannot think of better representatives for the Kingdom than the Yohes who we can journey alongside."
Ellen Pollock – Director of Congregational Care Ministry, New Covenant United Methodist Church, The Villages, FL

➤ "The beauty of what happens in a Hope for Hurting Parents support group has been so inspiring to us at Village View Church. The group is a safe place for participants to take their hurt, let it out, then leave with the hope they need to make it through another day with the strength of Jesus Christ guiding every step."
Deb Williams – former Recovery and Support Ministries Pastor, Village View Community Church, Summerfield, FL

➤ "Tom and Dena Yohe have lived through the ups and downs, and hurts and joys of life with a prodigal. All they have learned is now helping so many others through their wonderful ministry, Hope for Hurting Parents. They not only have wise encouragement, but also powerful prayers."
Judy Douglass - Writer, Speaker, Encourager, Founder Prayer for Prodigals Campus Crusade for Christ, International (Cru)

➤ "I would like to recommend Tom and Dena Yohe's ministry, Hope for Hurting Parents. In the words of one of the parents attending their small group, 'I just love these two people. They have helped me so much to understand my role as a parent. I felt like I was really helped. It really is important that I attend these sessions.' "
Pastor Marty Shea - Senior Pastor, Village View Community Church, Summerfield, FL

Mental Health Professionals

- "Tom and Dena are passionate and devoted to their cause. They can personally identify with parents who are struggling to raise and deal with difficult children. They also help families with adult children who are still problematic. I love what they are doing and want to continue to see their ministry grow so they can help as many hurting families as possible."
  Debbie Haughton - Licensed Mental Health Counselor, Orlando Counseling Services, Orlando, FL

- "These support groups provide a safe place to feel, share, and encourage one another as hurting parents who are on a journey through parenting challenges with adolescent or adult children. The groups are warm, intimate and confidential. The facilitators guide parents with hope through their many resources. I often refer hurting parents to Hope for Hurting Parents as it is a crucial piece of the healing process. I'm excited to see this group multiply and bless others!"
  Tanya Alvarado, MA, LMHC, New Path Counseling, Orlando, FL

- "No one should suffer alone. This support group was designed to come alongside of hurting parents. It is safe and parents can come with their authentic selves to receive love and support without judgement. I know of no other group like it. I personally have felt buoyed up and prayed for during some of my most difficult parenting days and continue to find those who supported me a continued support today. It is a gift to carry one another's burdens and share in their pain side by side. It is an experience of Jesus being present to heal the brokenhearted."
  Nancy A. Johnson, EdD, LMHC

- "As a parent of two sons who struggle with mental health concerns, I personally know the value of a caring, knowledgeable support network. This group provides that and more. The discussions are open and honest; the information shared is practical and understandable; the relationships formed are invaluable. I highly recommend this group to my clients who are parents seeking to love their child well in the difficult times."
  Mike Wilcox, M.A., M.A., LMHC, Pinnacle Counseling Institute, Orlando, FL

Session 1

GRIEF AND LOSS

GRIEF AND LOSS

Session Aim:

Parents will recognize they are grieving, identify what they've lost, understand how it may be affecting them, and learn how to grieve in a healthy way.

Key Principles:

Grief is a normal reaction to having a rebellious child. Whatever you're feeling is okay. Talk about it and reach out to others who understand for help.

Scripture:

Psalm 34:18

"The LORD is close to the brokenhearted and saves those who are crushed in spirit."

2 Corinthians 1:3–4

"Praise be to the God and Father of our Lord Jesus Christ, the Father of compassion and the God of all comfort, who comforts us in all our troubles, so that we can comfort those in any trouble with the comfort we ourselves receive from God."

Proverbs 17:22

"A cheerful heart is good medicine, but a crushed spirit dries up the bones."

Revelation 21:4

"He will wipe every tear from their eyes. There will be no more death or mourning or crying or pain, for the old order of things has passed away."

Materials Needed:

One index card for each person.

Resources:

Grief Share www.griefshare.org

Hope of a Homecoming by O'Rourke and Sauer, chapter 8

Parents with Broken Hearts by William Coleman, chapter 3

On Death and Dying by Elisabeth Kubler-Ross

The Other Side of Sadness by George A. Bonanno, chapters 3, 4, 6, and 12

Session: GRIEF AND LOSS

*Note to facilitator: another study on bereavement by George Bonanno is explained in his book *The Other Side of Sadness*. While not written from a Christian worldview, it is insightful because of a surprising element—*laughter*. It might sound irreverent. However, if you reflect on your own personal experiences with grief and loss, it may resonate. When you remember the good times and think about lighter moments with your loved one, smiles and even laughter can come. It's like coming up for air, catching your breath during a difficult time. This not only helps those who are grieving; it also helps those wanting to offer comfort to the bereaved individual, since it disarms some of the awkwardness in painful situations.

In the midst of our support group discussions, we often experience spontaneous laughter. Even in great pain we've found ourselves laughing together. At times we laughed so hard it brought tears to our eyes. It felt so good.

Introduction

Say, "*In today's session we're going to discuss grief and loss. We'll begin by defining grief and looking at its stages. Then we'll use three questions to help us process our grief: What have we lost? What do we have left? How can we cope?*"

Definition

Ask, "*How would you define grief?*" *Wait for their answers. Then ask someone to read the dictionary definition below.*

Dictionary.com definition: "keen mental suffering or distress over affliction or loss; sharp sorrow; painful regret." It is a normal emotional response to significant loss, not only from death; the loss of health (diabetes, cancer, etc.), a job, miscarriage, or divorce. The process of adjustment to a major loss; processed differently for each person (personality, past experiences, etc.).

Read *the following paragraphs to the group.*

Hurting parents experience grief and loss too; not necessarily from death, but from the loss of relationship, the loss of dreams and hopes they had for their son or daughter. People experience a wide range of feelings and symptoms.

Five Stages of Grief

Say, "Psychiatrist, Elisabeth Kubler-Ross, author of *On Death and Dying*, popularized a five-stage model of grieving." ***Ask*** *a volunteer to read the stages.*

1. Shock (I can't believe this is happening.)
2. Denial (My child wouldn't do that.); Bargaining (God, I'll do _____ if you'll do _____.)
3. Anger (Why is this happening to me? What did we do wrong?)
4. Depression (I'm too sad to go to work. Will I ever laugh again?)
5. Acceptance (I'm at peace with what has happened or whatever is going to happen.)

Grief is a process that takes time.

It's possible to skip around and revisit these stages. At times you may feel: numb, guilty, anxious, fearful, unable to focus or concentrate, a desire to withdraw, irritable, more forgetful, extreme fatigue, restless, health problems worsen or develop new ones.

Possible physical symptoms: dizziness, rapid heartbeat, a lump or tightness in your throat, pressure on your chest, headaches, sleeplessness, loss of appetite, or increased appetite.

Ask, *"Which of these have you felt?"*

Optional Question: Where are you on your grief journey?

Three Questions to Help Process Grief

Give *each person an index card.* ***Ask*** *questions one and two, one at a time.*

1. **What have you lost?**

   Ask the question, allowing them a few minutes to think and write down their responses on one side of the index card. Let those who want to share losses they identified. After several have shared, ask a volunteer to read the list of examples.

   Possible answers: hopes and dreams you had for your child; what might have been, graduate from high school or college; have a good job; get married; grandchildren; a loving, close relationship; financial resources (counseling, rehab, doctors, lawyers, fees, etc.); possessions (things get borrowed, disappear or end up in a pawn shop); time from work; sleep; your health; some friendships; peace of mind; your marriage; relationships with other children; your reputation. If you aren't careful you can even lose your faith.

2. **What do you have left?**

   Ask the question, allowing them a few minutes to think and write down their responses on the other side of the index card. Let those who want to share what they have left. After several have shared, ask a volunteer to read the list of examples.

   Possible answers: your other relationships—spouse, other children, friends; your relationship with God; your work and hobbies; your life—you do still have one. You have purpose. How can you use this for good?

   After discussion, read this statement to the group: "Don't let your child become the sole focus of your world. You have to get on with living your life with joy and peace again."

3. **How can you cope?**

   Read, "Here are three steps to help you grieve in a healthy way." Ask volunteers to take turns reading the following content:

   • Learn to accept that your loss is real and you are grieving.

     - You have lost something significant and important.

     - You can't get it back; your life has changed forever; you will never be the same.

     - Take time to remember good memories from the past; it wasn't all bad.

- Give yourself permission to feel the pain.

  - It's emotional and physical; you can't avoid it; don't stuff it or deny it. Let yourself feel the pain and get it out. Denying can make you sick or prolong the grieving process.

  - It's okay to distract yourself, but not for too long—working longer hours, staying busy, eating more.

  - Don't minimize it or seek to escape it—sleeping more or self-medicating.

  - Talk to a trusted friend, keep a journal if you like to write, express yourself in creative ways if you have this talent.

- Adjust to your new normal.

  - Shift your focus to other people and healthy activities.

  - Try to keep doing your normal, daily tasks as much as you can.

  - Give yourself permission to cry or be angry; feel whatever you're feeling. It's okay.

  - Talk about how you feel; don't let others tell you how you should feel.

  - Take care of yourself—exercise, take naps if needed, eat healthy, and get adequate rest.

  - Ask for help if you need it—see a counselor or your pastor; go to your doctor for a checkup; you may need medication temporarily.

George Bonanno states in his book *The Other Side of Sadness*, "Grieving is not static but involves a regular oscillation." These are periods or cycles when you fluctuate in and out of laughter, even joy, in the midst of the waves of sadness. Positive emotions and smiling bring some relief. While it sounds contradictory, his research found that those who have this capacity will grieve in a healthier way and be more resilient.

Read, *"It's important to learn to grieve well because it's critical to our survival and finding joy in hard times. Otherwise we will live in defeat and lose our joy."*

Scripture

Ask volunteers to read these verses.

Psalm 34:18

"The LORD is close to the brokenhearted and saves those who are crushed in spirit."

2 Corinthians 1:3–4

"Praise be to the God and Father of our Lord Jesus Christ, the Father of compassion and the God of all comfort, who comforts us in all our troubles, so that we can comfort those in any trouble with the comfort we ourselves receive from God."

Proverbs 17:22

"A cheerful heart is good medicine, but a crushed spirit dries up the bones."

Revelation 21:4

"He will wipe every tear from their eyes. There will be no more death or mourning or crying or pain, for the old order of things has passed away.

Reflection

Ask, *"What stood out the most for you from our discussion?*

Prayer

NOTES

Session 2

ENABLING

ENABLING

Session Aim:

To help parents understand the difference between helping and enabling, identify their enabling behaviors, and break the enabling cycle.

Key Principles:

While it may feel like love and loyalty, enabling allows an individual to avoid experiencing the natural consequences of their actions. Enabling actually makes it easier for them to get worse by reinforcing irresponsible behaviors and dependence. Parents can help things get better when they stop enabling.

Scripture:

Hebrews 12:11
"For the moment all discipline seems painful rather than pleasant, but later it yields the peaceful fruit of righteousness to those who have been trained by it."

Joshua 1:9 ESV
"Have I not commanded you? Be strong and courageous. Do not be frightened, and do not be dismayed, for the LORD your God is with you wherever you go."

Philippians 4:13 NKJV
"I can do all things through Christ who strengthens me."

2 Timothy 1:7 CEV
"God's Spirit doesn't make cowards out of us. The Spirit gives us power, love, and self-control."

Resources:

Setting Boundaries with Your Adult Children by Allison Bottke
Codependent No More by Melodie Beattie

Ready? Set? Go! by Judy Hampton

Codependency, Celebrate Recovery Literature

Courage to Change, February 1 Reading, Al-Anon Literature

Session: ENABLING

Introduction

Say to the group, *"In our discussion today we're going to discuss enabling. We'll define it, understand how it's different from helping, discover why we do it, and learn how we can break the enabling cycle."*

Enabling or Helping

Ask, and encourage sharing, *"What is your understanding of enabling?"*

Say, *"Let's look at some definitions for enabling and see how it's different from helping."*

Ask volunteers to read.

1. Enabling is reacting to a person in such a way to shield them from experiencing the full impact of harmful consequences of their behavior. Enabling differs from helping in that it permits or allows the person to be irresponsible (Celebrate Recovery).

2. Enabling is doing for someone what they could and should do for themselves. Helping is doing something for someone they can't do for themselves.

Enabling Behaviors

Ask, *"Are you an enabling parent?"* After some discussion, refer them to the Enabling Survey in their Parent Notebook. Give them time to read and mark the behaviors they see in themselves.

Read, *"Change isn't easy. Our enabling behaviors may be a pattern we've had for a long time. We must decide what we're going to do. Remember, enabling may help our children deny their deep problems. If we've played a part, it must stop."*

Ask a volunteer to read Hebrews 12:11

"For the moment all discipline seems painful rather than pleasant, but later it yields the peaceful fruit of righteousness to those who have been trained by it."

Why We Enable

Ask volunteers to read the list below, and then ask for comments.

As parents, we enable because:

- We have confused helping with enabling.
- We love too much, too little, and too conditionally.
- We fear for our child's safety, consequences, and the what-ifs.
- We feel guilty about what we did or didn't do.
- We never dealt with our own painful past, including abandonment, abuse, addictions, and other painful circumstances that made us who we are today.
- Our personality traits make us tend to do this.
- It's what we've been doing (habit).
- It's easier than changing.
- It feels like the right thing to do.
- We think our child is disabled or handicapped due to their addiction.
- We're short-sighted and don't know any better.

(Concepts from *Setting Boundaries with Your Adult Children* by Allison Bottke)

Identifying Our Own Issues

Read this statement, and *ask* the next two questions.

"We must ask ourselves these hard questions to understand why we enable. It will take courage to identify our own issues."

1. "What reward are you getting from enabling?"

2. "What need is this filling in your life?"

After discussion, ask volunteers to read these possible responses:

- I feel like I've been helpful.
- It makes me feel better.
- I need to be in control.
- It feels good.

- I like to help.

- I'm a fixer.

- It feels like loving—if I do this, maybe they'll respond back to me in a loving way.

- I think it will guarantee their acceptance. I feel more secure in our relationship.

- I'm protecting my pride and good reputation (and theirs)—if they fall I'll look like a bad parent. What will others think of me—of them?

Read, *"We need to work on being healthy ourselves. When we don't need to enable or feel rewarded for doing so, we'll find the strength to say, "No, I'm sorry_____, but I decided I can't or won't be helping you with that anymore. But I'm confident you will solve this problem on your own. You can do it!"*

Remember, when we stop enabling, those around us may change too, but there's no guarantee we'll like those changes. We need to stop enabling because it's the right thing for us to do, because it's best for us, not just because of how we hope it will affect our child."

Ask, *"Does anyone have a comment about what I just read?'*

Four Reminders:

Ask volunteers to take turns reading.

Change is not easy. We can pray for the power to change ourselves.

By not enabling we can help our children of any age develop wings to fly on their own.

We can find comfort in knowing we are not alone on this journey.

We can take back our lives.

Scripture

Ask the group to read these verses out loud together.

Joshua 1:9 ESV

"Have I not commanded you? Be strong and courageous. Do not be frightened, and do not be dismayed, for the LORD your God is with you wherever you go."

Philippians 4:13 NKJV

"I can do all things through Christ who strengthens me."

2 Timothy 1:7 CEV

"God's Spirit doesn't make cowards out of us. The Spirit gives us power, love, and self-control."

Reflection

Ask, *"What is your take-away from this session on enabling?"*

Prayer

ENABLING SURVEY

1. Have personal belongings mysteriously disappeared from your home?
2. Have you finished a project your child left undone because it was easier than asking them to do it?
3. Did you pay for education or job training more than once?
4. Does your child use profanity, violence, or other unacceptable behavior toward you without consequences?
5. Do you repeatedly give second chances?
6. Do you continuously loan them money and rarely get paid back?
7. Do you have concerns about your finances because of helping them?
8. Have you avoided talking about hard things because you're afraid of their reaction?
9. Are you worried about the damage to your marriage due to the strain from your child?
10. Has there been increased resentment from their siblings or other relatives?
11. Do you now, or have you paid your adult child's bills?
12. Do you pay their cell phone bill so you can contact them?
13. Have you bailed them out of jail or paid for a lawyer more than once?
14. Do they have money for nonessentials (cigarettes, tattoos, movies, etc.) yet need to borrow money from you?
15. Have you asked your adult child (who lives with you) to pay rent but they refuse?
16. Have you given ultimatums but didn't follow through?
17. Have you ever called in sick or made excuses for them?
18. Do you wonder why they can't get or keep a job?
19. Do you feel like there's nothing else you can do for them?
20. Are you mad at yourself for what you've been doing?

   *These are adapted from Allison Bottke's Enabling Survey in her book *Setting Boundaries with Your Adult Children*.

NOTES

Session 3

GUILT

GUILT

Session Aim:

Help participants distinguish between real and false guilt and move toward guilt-free parenting.

Key Principles:

Perfect parenting is no guarantee of raising perfect children. Parenting skills, good or bad, are not an excuse for our children's destructive decisions. God's forgiveness and grace can bring freedom.

Scripture:

Genesis 1:31; 3:6 ESV

"And God saw everything that he had made, and behold, it was very good. And there was evening and there was morning, the sixth day."

"So when the woman saw that the tree was good for food, and that it was a delight to the eyes, and that the tree was to be desired to make one wise, she took of its fruit and ate, and she also gave some to her husband who was with her, and he ate."

Isaiah 1:2 ESV

"Hear, O heavens, and give ear, O earth; for the LORD has spoken: "Children have I reared and brought up, but they have rebelled against me."

Isaiah 5:1–4 ESV

"Let me sing for my beloved my love song concerning his vineyard: My beloved had a vineyard on a very fertile hill. He dug it and cleared it of stones, and planted it with choice vines; he built a watchtower in the midst of it, and hewed out a wine vat in it; and he looked for it to yield grapes, but it yielded wild grapes. And now, O inhabitants of Jerusalem and men of Judah, judge between me and my vineyard. What more was there to do for my vineyard that I have not done in it? When I looked for it to yield grapes, why did it yield wild grapes?"

Psalm 25:11 ESV

"For your name's sake, O LORD, pardon my guilt, for it is great."

Isaiah 6:7

"See, this has touched your lips; your guilt is taken away and your sin atoned for."

1 John 1: 9 ESV

"If we confess our sins, he is faithful and just to forgive us our sins and to cleanse us from all unrighteousness."

Romans 8:1 ESV

"There is therefore now no condemnation for those who are in Christ Jesus."

Ephesians 6:11

"Put on the full armor of God so that you can take your stand against the devil's schemes."

Resources:

Hope of a Homecoming by O'Rourke and Sauer, chapter 5

Parents with Broken Hearts by William Coleman, chapter 6

Will Your Prodigal Come Home by Jeff Lucas, chapter 7

Loving a Prodigal by H. Norman Wright, chapter 3

Session: GUILT

Introduction

Say to the group, *"In this session we're going to discuss guilt. We will define it, rate how guilty we feel, and discover what we can do about it."*

Ask a volunteer to read, *"We've all felt guilty at times over the situation with our child. It seems to be part of the "why" question. There must be some reason. Maybe it's my fault? We ask ourselves painful questions: "What did I do wrong?" "How could my child be this way?" "How could I have prevented this?"*

Ask a volunteer to read the definition.

Definition

A feeling of responsibility or remorse for some offense, crime, or wrong, etc. whether real or imagined. Self-reproach; self-blame; feeling at fault for something.

Read these instructions and encourage sharing, "Rate yourself on a scale of 1 to 10 (10 being the highest): how guilty do you feel today and why did you choose that number?"

The Perfect Parent

Read, "Even the best parents look for an explanation for their failures. They say, "If I'd only . . ." and "If I just hadn't . . ." On and on they examine their parenting record, looking for that moment, that mistake that flipped the switch in their relationship. Let's look at a parent who did it all perfectly and had no guilt."

Ask volunteers to read these Scripture verses and guide discussion using open-ended questions.

Genesis 1:31 and 3:6; Isaiah 1:2 and 5:1–4. *Note, these scriptures are written out in the beginning of this session.*

Ask, "What truths about parenting do you see in these passages?"

After discussion, ask a volunteer to read, "Perfect parenting does not guarantee results. We may even get an unexpected outcome. Parents with rebellious children are in good company. Even God's children rebelled."

Ask, "How does this truth affect your level of guilt?"

What Can We Do About Our Guilt?

Ask volunteers to read numbers 1 through 5.

1. Ask God to bring to mind any sin and confess it. Be honest without morbid introspection. He will forgive and remove your guilt. God may reveal that you need to ask your child for forgiveness; doing this can have a huge impact on them.

2. Find a safe person and honestly share your struggle with guilt.

3. Don't own your child's problems. Remember, they're making a choice. They are accountable to God for the things they do.

4. False guilt—there's no reason for it; own what you need to own and refuse the rest; learn to recognize Satan's lies; ask God to show you what they are and then to remove them.

5. Let go of the past and move forward; you can't change what has been done. Give yourself a lot of grace; you've never done this before; with God's help you're doing the best you can.

Scripture

Ask volunteers read the following verses:

Psalm 25:11; Isaiah 6:7; 1 John 1:9; Romans 8:1; and Ephesians 6:11

Note: These scriptures are written out for you in the beginning of this session.

Reflection

Ask, "What did you need most from this session?" Conclude by reading the **Key Principles** at the beginning of these notes.

Prayer

NOTES

Session 4

COPING WITH FEAR

COPING WITH FEAR

Session Aim:

To help parents identify their fears, begin facing them, and develop a strategy for coping.

Key Principles:

Fear is the number one enemy of broken-hearted parents. It steals their peace and makes them nervous wrecks. Learning to cope with their fears is crucial to restoring them to sanity.

Scripture:

Isaiah 43:1–5
"But now this is what the Lord says—he who created you . . . he who formed you . . . 'Do not fear, for I have redeemed you; I have summoned you by name; you are mine. When you pass through the waters, I will be with you; and when you pass through the rivers, they will not sweep over you. When you walk through the fire, you will not be burned; the flames will not set you ablaze. For I am the Lord your God, the Holy One of Israel, your Savior. . . . Since you are precious and honored in my sight, and because I love you . . . Do not be afraid, for I am with you.' "

Psalm 23:4
"Even though I walk through the darkest valley, I will fear no evil, for you are with me; your rod and your staff, they comfort me."

Psalm 27:3 ESV

"Though an army encamp against me, my heart shall not fear; though war rise against me, yet I will be confident."

Psalm 46:1

"God is our refuge and strength, an ever-present help in trouble."

1 John 4:18

"There is no fear in love. But perfect love drives out fear, because fear has to do with punishment. The one who fears has not been made perfect in love."

Isaiah 41:10 ESV

"Fear not, for I am with you; be not dismayed, for I am your God; I will strengthen you, I will help you, I will uphold you with my righteous right hand."

Materials Needed:

Provide a sheet of paper for each participant and a small trash can or large bowl. Depending on how you choose to have participants destroy their fear list you may need scissors. See the **Individual Activity on page 48.**

Resources:

Hope for a Homecoming by O'Rourke and Sauer, chapter 6
Don't Let Your Kids Kill You by Charles Rubin, chapter 5

Session: FEAR

Introduction

Say, *"In our discussion today we're going to discuss fear. We'll define it, identify our own fears, begin facing them by looking at how they affect us, and learn how we can cope better."*

Read: *Fear is Satan's best weapon against us. It is our number one enemy. It ties us up in knots, paralyzes us, weakens our faith, robs us of peace and joy, and causes us to enable our children. It causes us to believe Satan's lies and forget what is true. It's one of our biggest problems as hurting parents.*

Ask *and wait for responses, "What do you think?"*

Ask *a volunteer to read the definition of fear and the acrostic below it.*

Definition

A distressing emotion aroused by impending danger, evil, pain, etc., whether the threat is real or imagined; the feeling or condition of being afraid. Synonyms: foreboding, apprehension, consternation, dismay, dread, terror, fright, panic, horror, trepidation, qualm (dictionary.com). It causes us to be nervous, worried, and anxious. It's one of the four major emotions—mad, sad, glad, and scared.

An acrostic: **False Evidence Appearing Real**

Identifying Our Fears

Give *everyone a sheet of paper. Then* **ask**, *"What are some things you fear for your child?"*

Instruct the group to write down everything they can think of that they are afraid of for their child, all of their "what-ifs." Give them a few minutes. Encourage sharing their list with the group.

Tell *them to hold on to their list for now.*

Ask, *"How does fear affect you?"* (physically, emotionally, relationally, and spiritually) *then encourage discussion.*

Possible answers: inability to sleep; loss of appetite or overeating; feeling anxious, nervous, and stressed; physical illness—ulcers, headaches, intestinal problems, chest pain; more emotional than usual; less patient, more irritable, shorter fuse; become more controlling with your child; begin enabling to protect; can be consumed by fear; can't stop thinking about it or talking about it; absorbs all of your thoughts; it takes over; may feel a need to self-medicate for relief (alcohol, nicotine, coffee, sugar); turn to forms of escape—TV, reading, internet, work, hobbies (not necessarily harmful things).

How We Cope

Read, *"Let's talk about how you can cope with your fears."*

Ask *and encourage discussion, "What helps you cope?"*

Ask *volunteers to read.*

- Think positively: "I'm going to be okay." "It could be worse." "I'm not alone."

- Focus on what you can be thankful for instead of the negative.

- Read Psalm 23 before bed, especially verse 2, "He makes me lie down in green pastures."

- Prayer: Keep a prayer journal and record answers; this increases your faith.

- Remind yourself God loves your child more than you do. He's not finished.

- Be honest about your fearful feelings. Verbalize your fears to yourself or someone else.

Coping Suggestions

Ask *volunteers to read number 1 through 5. Pause to ask for comments and thoughts after each section.*

1. Feed your faith

   Faith thrives on truth and makes it grow stronger. Read scripture, memorize verses, listen to uplifting music, read helpful books, attend worship services, etc.

2. Focus on truth

   God is with us; we are not alone; He will help us; He wants to help our child; He's able to do the impossible; He will never stop trying to reach them; He will use everything for good in their lives and in ours. Search the scriptures for verses that address fear and fill your mind with them. Here's a great one:

   "But now, this is what the LORD says—he who created you . . . he who formed you . . .

   Do not fear, for I have redeemed you;

   I have summoned you by name, you are mine.

   When you pass through the waters, I will be with you;

   and when you pass through the rivers (at flood stage), they will not sweep over you.

   When you walk through the fire (of affliction and suffering), you will not be burned;

   the flames will not set you ablaze.

   For I am the LORD your God, the Holy One of Israel, your Savior . . .

   Since you are precious and honored in my sight, and because I love you . . .

   Do not be afraid, for I am with you (Isaiah 43:1–5a)."

3. Avoid fantasy faith

   Convincing ourselves everything will be fine, it's going to be okay, nothing bad is going to happen, she won't get pregnant, he won't end up in jail, they won't become an alcoholic, etc.

Something bad could happen. We don't know what the outcome will be. We have no guarantees our child will survive or return home safely.

4. Let fear draw you closer to God

We learn to rely more, trust more, pray more, read the Bible more, and attend worship services. Do everything we can to spiritually strengthen ourselves.

5. Face your fears

- Facing our fears disarms them. They no longer have as much power over us.

- Remember God is with us in it. Take Him into this part of our journey.

- Here's a good slogan: "Fear knocked on the door. Faith answered and no one was there!"

- Ask yourself, "What does God have for me in this fearful time?"

- Accept the what-ifs and make peace with them.

- You may need the help of a professional counselor or minister.

Individual Activity

Say, "*Take out the list of fears you made earlier. We're going to take a few minutes for private, personal prayer and we're going to give those fears to God. When you feel ready, destroy your list. Then drop the pieces into this container.*"

*Be creative with ideas for how they destroy their list. For example, if you have a fireplace or fire pit you could use that—i.e. they could throw their papers into the fire and watch them burn. You could provide scissors to cut up them up or they could tear and rip them. Provide a small trash can or large bowl for them to throw the pieces of paper into.

Suggestions to try at home

If you have time, **ask** *a volunteer to read these.*

- Pray for God to help you trust Him with your fears instead of dwelling on them.

- Pray for reassurance of His presence.

- Pray for increased faith and how you can feed yours.

- Spend more time praying than being fearful. Use the scriptures for your prayers.

- Find a prayer partner who has experienced being fearful over a wayward child.

- Read John 14:27; Jesus gives you His peace and tells you not to be afraid.

Prayer

NOTES

Session 5

DETACHMENT

DETACHMENT

Session Aim:

To clarify the meaning of detachment, how to apply it in the context of unhealthy relationships, and how to cope with the feelings it brings.

Key Principles:

By learning to detach, the parent's attitude and well-being will improve.

Scripture:

John 21:21–22
"When Peter saw him, he asked, 'Lord, what about him?' Jesus answered, 'If I want him to remain alive until I return, what is that to you? You must follow me.'"

Joshua 1:9
"Have I not commanded you? Be strong and courageous. Do not be afraid; do not be discouraged, for the LORD your God will be with you wherever you go."

Ephesians 6:10
"Finally, be strong in the LORD and in his mighty power."

Resources:

Courage to Change, Al-Anon literature

One Day at a Time, Al-Anon literature

Co-Dependent No More by Melodie Beattie, chapter 5

Session: DETACHMENT

Introduction

Ask, "What do you think about the concept of detachment? How does it make you feel? Is it helpful, confusing, or not helpful?"

Definition

Have volunteers read. Ask for comments after each paragraph.

Definition

Indifferent, aloof, and withdrawn from; to be disconnected, disinterested, isolated, and unconcerned; avoiding emotional involvement. To unfasten and separate; disengage, disunite (dictionary.com).

These terms are perhaps the reason many parents feel detachment is confusing or even wrong. This is not what is meant when you hear, "We need to detach."

Detachment is neither kind nor unkind. It does not imply judgment or condemnation of the person from whom we are detaching. Separating ourselves from the adverse effects of another person's destructive behaviors is detaching.

This doesn't always require physical separation. Detachment is not separating from the person we care about, but from the agony of our involvement with them. Detachment can help us be more objective about the situation.

Recovery proponents teach there is nothing we can say or do to cause or stop a person's destructive behavior. We're not responsible for our child's problems or their recovery from them. Detachment allows us to let go of our obsession with our child so we can have healthier lives—lives with dignity, guided by God. We can still love them without liking their behavior.

Through Detachment We Can Learn

Ask volunteers to read and discuss.

- Not to suffer because of the actions or reactions of other people.

- Not to allow ourselves to be used or abused by others in the interest of their recovery.

- Not to do for others what they can do for themselves.

- Not to manipulate situations so others will eat, go to bed, get up, pay bills, not drink or use drugs, or behave the way we want them to.

- Not to cover up for someone else's mistakes or failures.

- Not to prevent a crisis if one happens as life unfolds.

Things to Remember

Ask volunteers to read, and then discuss one paragraph at a time.

The process of detaching is stressful for everyone in the family because human nature usually sees significant change as stressful. It can be just as difficult for us to change our own patterns of behavior as it is for our child. Old habits die hard.

Learning to detach brings another new reality: a letting go of our attempts to control, of denying our own feelings and needs, and of the false belief that our child has to be okay before we can be okay. These changes cause an upheaval in the family system. Everyone must readjust.

Living with the effects of someone else's destructive behavior is too much for most people to bear alone. The feeling of powerlessness over our child can cause us to feel overwhelmed by fear, helplessness, grief, confusion, and a lack of understanding. We don't know what to do next.

Reading helpful materials, attending support groups, meeting with a counselor, and practicing other self-care actions can lessen this stress.

By learning to focus on ourselves, allowing our loved one to experience the consequences of their own actions, our well-being will improve. This can be hard. We'll need a lot of courage.

Have the group read the following two verses in unison.

Joshua 1:9
"Have I not commanded you? Be strong and courageous. Do not be afraid; do not be discouraged, for the LORD your God will be with you wherever you go."

Ephesians 6:10
"Finally, be strong in the LORD and in his mighty power."

Reflection

Ask, "In light of this session, how has your understanding of detachment changed? What did you need most from this content?"

Prayer

NOTES

Session 6

WORRY AND ANXIETY

WORRY AND ANXIETY

Session Aim:

To help parents realize it doesn't make sense to worry themselves sick about things that are out of their control and discover steps they can take to regain peace of mind.

Key Principles:

Worry is unproductive; it can make us sick, hurt relationships, and affects our ability to make decisions. Prayer, gratitude, and trust are antidotes for worry.

Scripture:

Matthew 6:25, 27, 33–34 NASB

"Do not be worried about your life. . . . Who of you by being worried can add a single hour to his life? . . . But seek first His kingdom and His righteousness, and all these things will be added to you. So do not worry about tomorrow; for tomorrow will care for itself. Each day has enough trouble of its own."

Philippians 4:6–7

"Do not be anxious about anything, but in every situation, by prayer and petition, with thanksgiving, present your requests to God. And the peace of God, which transcends all understanding, will guard your hearts and your minds in Christ Jesus."

1 Peter 5:7

"Cast all your anxiety on him because he cares for you."

Psalm 94:19

"When anxiety was great within me, your consolation brought me joy."

Resources:

CareNotes booklet on Worry by Abbey Press. For a complete catalog of Caring publications visit www.carenotes.com

Session: WORRY AND ANXIETY

Introduction

Read *the following two paragraphs. They are also in the parent notebook.*

It doesn't make sense to worry yourself sick about things that are not in your control. Worry gives a false sense of control over something we can't do anything about.

Not all of life's troubles have a happy ending. Sometimes there's good reason to be anxious. Worry is a common response. Sometimes we can't stop; it becomes chronic; even obsessive. It can get out of control. Then our ability to think clearly and make good decisions is compromised. Here are a few steps to help regain peace of mind.

Ask *volunteers to read one section at a time and discuss.*

Four Steps to Help Regain Peace of Mind

1. Make a physical change

    • The next time you feel yourself worrying uncontrollably, stop and look in a mirror. Notice the tension in your forehead and eyes, your clenched jaw, frown, and stooped posture. Worry takes a toll on our bodies.

    • Breathe deeply. Take a deep breath and another one. Deep and slow. In through your nose, out through your mouth. It will slow your pulse, clear your mind, and relax your muscles. When we worry we tend to hold our breath. We take shallow, short breaths, which heightens anxiety. Give yourself more oxygen—it can do wonderful things for your well-being and it's free.

    • Take a long walk, then a warm bath or shower. Connecting with the beauty of nature is relaxing. Direct your gaze upward and really look at the sky. Let it remind you how great God is. Aerobic exercise and getting a massage are other ways to release worry. Discover what you like and make yourself do it.

2. Change things or change your attitude

   • Realize that being anxious about someone you have no control over won't make them change. It's wasted energy. It can't add even a day to our lives (Matthew 6:27).

   • Try to change something you can—your attitude. Change negative self-talk—"Not this again." "Why does it always have to happen?" "Just what I was afraid of." "They'll never change."—into positive self-talk. Otherwise you'll remain trapped in the problem.

   • Supportive self-talk is a healthier remedy. Replace anxious thoughts with truth and positive thoughts: "I know God will help me." "This too shall pass." "With God's help I can handle whatever comes." "Somehow it will all work out." "Let go and let God."

   • Use laughter and humor as a distraction. Watch a funny movie or call someone who uplifts you.

   • If you're in a "worrywart rut," listen to soothing music or listen to something encouraging.

3. Turn it over

   • Prayer and meditation on God and His Word can soothe your mind and soul. Instead of worrying, pray. Let your worry be your prayer. We know we need to give it to God, but how slow we are to do it.

   • Let go of your worries by handing them over to God. There's nothing we can do about them, but we can give them to the One who can do something.

   • Philippians 4:6–7 says, "Do not be anxious about anything, but in everything, by prayer and petition, with thanksgiving, present your requests to God. And the peace of God, which transcends all understanding, will guard your hearts and your minds in Christ Jesus."

   • Make an exchange—your worry for God's peace.

4. Move outside yourself in gratitude and trust

   • Look for someone you can help. A small act of kindness can boost your spirit and distract you from your own troubles. It also has a way of reminding you of your blessings.

- Gratitude is another good antidote for worry. It's rather difficult to worry and be grateful at the same time! Making a list of what we can be thankful for helps keep our worries in their proper perspective.

- Trust is another key to overcoming worry. Ask God to help you trust Him more, as well as yourself and the supportive people around you. Bad things do happen, but we can trust and be confident that whatever happens, we will have or be given by God what we need to handle the situation.

Scripture

Ask *volunteers to read the scripture verses.*

Matthew 6:25, 27, 33–34 NASB
"Do not be worried about your life. . . . Who of you by being worried can add a single hour to his life? . . . But seek first His kingdom and His righteousness, and all these things will be added to you. So do not worry about tomorrow; for tomorrow will care for itself. Each day has enough trouble of its own."

Philippians 4:6–7
"Do not be anxious about anything, but in everything, by prayer and petition, with thanksgiving, present your requests to God. And the peace of God, which transcends all understanding, will guard your hearts and your minds in Christ Jesus."

1 Peter 5:7
"Cast all your anxiety on him because he cares for you."

Psalm 94:19
"When anxiety was great within me, your consolation brought me joy."

Reflection

Ask, *"What is your take-away from this session?"*

Prayer

NOTES

Session 7

ANGER

ANGER

Session Aim:

To define anger, accept feelings of anger, and learn how to express them in healthy ways.

Key Principles:

Anger is a valid emotional response. It matters what we do with it because anger has the potential to damage our relationships.

Scripture:

Ephesians 4:26
"In your anger do not sin; do not let the sun go down while you are still angry."

James 1:19-20 ESV
"Know this, my beloved brothers: let every person be quick to hear, slow to speak, slow to anger; for the anger of man does not produce the righteousness of God."

Proverbs 15:1 ESV
"A soft answer turns away wrath, but a harsh word stirs up anger."

Resources:

Surviving a Prodigal: Studies for Parents of Prodigals by Crider and Wamberg, session 3

Session: ANGER

Introduction

Ask this question and encourage discussion. "How was anger viewed in the family you grew up in, and how has that affected you today?"

Read, *"Many of us react without thinking when confronted with the unacceptable choices of our rebellious child. Sadly, our emotional responses do very little to help the situation. Let's define anger and some of its consequences."*

Ask, "How do you define anger?"

Have a volunteer read the definition of anger in the Parent Notebook, the following paragraph, and James 1:19–20.

Definition

A strong feeling of displeasure and belligerence aroused by a wrong; irritation or aggravation (dictionary.com).

Some of us tend to tone it down and say we're frustrated when we are really mad. It's okay to be angry. Psychologists say it is one of the four main emotions—mad, sad, glad, and scared. It's what we do with our feelings of anger that's important. This also applies to anger we may feel toward God. He already knows if we are and He's big enough to take it.

James 1:19–20
"Know this, my beloved brothers: let every person be quick to hear, slow to speak, slow to anger; for the anger of man does not produce the righteousness of God."

Have them turn to the Anger Worksheet in their Parent Notebook. Have the group answer the questions on their own. After about five minutes, encourage sharing their answers with the group. Here are the three questions on the worksheet:

How would you describe yourself when you're angry?

In what ways does your child make you mad?

What can happen when our anger is out of control?

Finding the Source of Our Anger

Ask a volunteer to read the following paragraph.

Our anger can be the result of our inability to be in control of other people's choices and actions. How often have you had this attitude: if only they would listen to my advice and do what I say, these things would not be happening. The scriptures warn us, "In your anger do not sin; do not let the sun go down while you are still angry" (Ephesians 4:26). God wants us to sort through our anger, find its source, and learn how to handle it.

Facilitate group discussion around the following questions. Don't feel you have to cover them all.

1. In what ways does your child make you mad?

2. What do you think is the underlying issue?

3. What do you have control over?

4. What changes would you like to make?

The Five Steps to Handling Anger

Ask volunteers to read Proverbs 15:1 and the Five Steps to Handling Anger. If you are short on time, read them without discussion.

"A soft answer turns away wrath, but a harsh word stirs up anger" (Proverbs 15:1).

1. Acknowledge that you're angry.

2. When you feel angry, don't resort to your typical negative response.

3. Find the focus of your anger. Ask yourself, "Why am I angry?"

4. Think about your options. How can you respond in a constructive way?

5. Take constructive action to resolve your anger.

Peaceful Discussion Guide

Say, "There is a Peaceful Discussion Guide in their Parent Notebook. We're not going to discuss it but you can read it on your own."

Reflection

Ask, "What helped you the most from this session?"

Prayer

PEACEFUL DISCUSSION GUIDE

1. Whenever possible, plan when and where you will talk.

2. Write down what the issues are.

3. Agree ahead of time to not attack each other personally. If one of you begins to attack, stop the discussion.

4. Agree that either person can call a time-out to regain control of their emotions. Choose a specific amount of time. This gives a chance to cool down and refocus.

5. If tempers begin to flare, a good phrase to memorize is, "Honey, I'm not the enemy."

6. Don't be caught by surprise. When you're approached unexpectedly, simply tell the other person you're not prepared to talk. Agree on a time and place for a discussion.

7. Be honest and show respect. The goal is to have peaceful discussions, not to win an argument.

8. Think about how you can end the discussion. For example: "I hear what you're saying and I'll think about it."

9. Before your discussion, try to call a trusted friend and ask them to pray that you'll listen well and not say anything hurtful.

10. Write down decisions or agreements you make to avoid confusion in the future.

NOTES

Session 8

RESENTMENT

RESENTMENT

Session Aim:

To discover what resentment is, how it manifests itself, the reasons parents may feel resentful, and how to cope.

Key Principles:

Resentment is an emotion of deep anger and bitterness. Forgiveness is essential to overcome feeling resentful.

Scripture:

Mark 11:25

"And when you stand praying, if you hold anything against anyone, forgive them, so that your Father in heaven may forgive you your sins."

Luke 6:28

"Bless those who curse you, pray for those who mistreat you."

2 Timothy 2:24

"And the Lord's servant must not be quarrelsome but must be kind to everyone, able to teach, not resentful."

Job 5:2

"Resentment kills a fool, and envy slays the simple."

Job 36:13

"The godless in heart harbor resentment."

Colossians 3:13 ESV

"Bearing with one another and, if one has a complaint against another, forgiving each other; as the Lord has forgiven you, so you also must forgive."

Resources:

Courage to Change and One Day at a Time, Al Anon literature

Session: RESENTMENT

Introduction

Have parents turn to this session in their notebooks and read the definition.

Definition

Resentment is "a feeling of indignant displeasure or persistent ill will at something regarded as a wrong, insult, or injury" (merriam-webster.com). An emotion of deep anger or bitterness as a result of being wronged; angry at having been mistreated or personally offended; betrayal of trust. Cold anger buried within as a result of being hurt.

Ask, "Which words stand out to you and why?"

How Resentment Manifests Itself

Ask volunteers to read and encourage discussion.

Resentment will often manifest itself in the following ways:

- Strong, aching emotional turmoil felt whenever a certain person or event is discussed.

- The lack of forgiving; the unwillingness to let go and forget.

- A root of distrust and suspicion when dealing with people or events that caused pain in the past.

- Unresolved grief, experienced when finding it difficult to accept a loss.

- A grudge held against a person, or group of people, by whom the person in question feels they've been kept from accomplishing something.

- It can be an emotionally disturbing experience that is repeatedly felt or replayed in the mind.

Reasons Parents May Feel Resentment Toward Their Child/Children

Ask volunteers to read the list below. Direct them to pair up with another person and share which ones they have felt. Allow three to five minutes.

- The emotional pain they have caused us.

- Loss of time away from work.

- Caring for/helping them has cost us money we didn't have—we may now have added debt.

- We feel taken advantage of, used, and rejected.

- Our health has suffered.

- Our marriage has suffered—stress and strain leading to increased conflict.

- Relationships with other children have suffered—increased conflict.

- Loss of reputation—our peers may think less of us.

- Time spent in counseling/psychiatrists/support groups (like this one!) we'd rather spend elsewhere. We resent that we have to take the time to be there.

- Having to raise and care for our grandchildren instead of enjoying retirement.

- Shattered expectations—their peers are moving ahead with their lives (careers, marriage, family) while our child is still dysfunctional and can't even hold down a job.

Ask, *"What could you add to this list?"*

A Few Ideas for Coping

Ask *volunteers to read and discuss.*

- Keep a journal.

- Talk to someone who will listen well and pray with you.

- Limit the amount of time you allow yourself to think about these things.

- Let go and let God.

- Ultimately, we must forgive. If we hold on to resentment we only hurt ourselves. Christ is our example. Forgive as He forgave us. "Bearing with one another and, if one has a complaint against another, forgiving each other; as the Lord has forgiven you, so you also must forgive" (Colossians 3:13).

- When we hold on to resentment, we only hurt ourselves. Practice forgiveness instead.

- Pray for them and ourselves. "Pray for those who mistreat you" (Luke 6:28).

Ask God, "Take the resentment out of me. Bless _____ in any and every way that seems best to you."

As we pray this way our attitude changes and sometimes theirs does too.

- Say encouraging things to them instead of being critical or nagging.

- Read encouraging things that uplift you and give hope.

Reflection

Ask, *"What new coping idea will you try to use?"*

Prayer

NOTES

Session 9

LETTING GO

LETTING GO

Session Aim:

To clarify what "letting go" is and what it is not, using the Serenity Prayer to help in the process.

Key Principles:

As our children get older or move out of our home, control is more of an illusion. Letting go can be the most loving thing for a parent to do because it allows our children to learn consequences of their own choices and helps us regain peace of mind.

Scripture:

I Peter 5:7
"Cast all your anxiety on him, because he cares for you."

Psalm 55:22 ESV
"Cast your burden on the Lord and he will sustain you."

Proverbs 3:5–6
"Trust in the Lord with all your heart and lean not on your own understanding; in all your ways submit to him, and he will make your paths straight."

Resources:

National Alliance on Mental Illness (NAMI), nami.org
The Serenity Prayer by Reinhold Niebuhr

Session: LETTING GO

Introduction

Ask this question and encourage sharing.

"Is letting go of your child difficult for you to do? Why or why not?"

Ask a volunteer to read this statement in their *Parent Notebook*, "Letting go can be difficult. It's similar to detaching, no longer trying to fix or change, but entrusting your loved one into God's hands. It's releasing your need to control, recognizing that only God has that power."

Let Go

Decide if you want volunteers to read each "Let Go" statement and discuss them one at a time, or read the entire list before discussion.

Author Unknown (words in parentheses indicate our additions).

To let go does not mean to stop caring. It means I can't do it for someone else.

To let go is not to cut myself off. It's the realization I can't control another.

To let go is to allow someone to learn from natural consequences.

To let go is to recognize when the outcome is not in my hands.

To let go is not to care for, but to care about.

To let go is not to fix, but to be supportive (by listening, empathizing, and finding ways to show you care without doing too much for them—enabling).

To let go is not to judge, but to allow another to be a human being.

To let go is not to expect (demand) miracles, but to take each day as it comes, and cherish myself in it. (To wrestle with the tension between expecting and believing God can do anything—He is the miracle worker—yet accepting what is.)

To let go is not to criticize or regulate anybody, but to try to become what I dream I can be.

To let go is not to regret the past, but to grow and live for the future. (Not to dwell on what has happened—it is what it is; we must accept our new normal. God made us very adaptable. We can do it with His strength. Look ahead with hope.)

To let go is to fear less and love more.

Scripture

Ask volunteers to read the scripture verses and the following paragraph. Allow for comments and discussion.

I Peter 5:7
"Cast all your anxiety on him, because he cares for you."

Psalm 55:22 ESV
"Cast your burden on the LORD, and he will sustain you."

Proverbs 3:5–6
"Trust in the Lord with all your heart and lean not on your own understanding; in all your ways submit to him, and he will make your paths straight."

We do not let go of our sons and daughters releasing them into nothingness. We release them into the hands of a loving and strong God. We let go to let God do His work of transformation and redemption.

Serenity Prayer

Read, "Many people have used the Serenity Prayer in the process of learning to let go. The focus is dealing with change."

Lead the group in reading the prayer in unison to conclude.

God grant me the serenity to accept the things I cannot change,

Courage to change the things I can,

And wisdom to know the difference.

Reflection

Ask, "What did you need most from this session?"

Prayer

NOTES

Session 10

EXPECTATIONS

EXPECTATIONS

Session Aim:

To understand that unfulfilled expectations can turn into anger and resentment. Contentment and peace of mind come from adjusting our expectations.

Key Principles:

When we feel resentful, we need to look at our expectations for a probable source. Adjusting expectations helps prevent setting ourselves up for constant disappointment. The best remedy is realistic acceptance of the situation.

Scripture:

Philippians 4:11

"I have learned to be content whatever the circumstances."

Romans 15:7

"Therefore, accept one another, just as Christ also accepted us to the glory of God."

Resources:

Courage to Change, Al-Anon literature

Session: EXPECTATIONS

Introduction

Read *the statement to the group then ask the following questions.*

"One source of frustration we seldom recognize is expecting too much of others or expecting too specifically what we feel they ought to be, say, give or do."

"What are some expectations you have of your child?"

"Have you experienced disappointment or anger toward them lately?"

"Can these emotions be traced back to expectations you had for their reactions or actions?"

Discussion

Ask a volunteer to read the following quote and invite discussion. Say, "What do you think?"

"An expectation is a premeditated resentment". Al-Anon

Remedies

Ask for volunteers to read the statements below. You can pause after each one for discussion, or wait until all have been read.

- When we experience resentment we need to look at our expectations.

- We have the right to choose our own standards of conduct, but we do not have the right to impose them on another person. As parents, we are responsible to teach and model certain standards of behavior to our children, but ultimately they have to choose. We can't choose for them.

- Every person has their own reasons for their behavior, beyond our understanding or control. We might say: "But she knew what I expected," not realizing that it may have been the very reason she rebelled and acted differently.

- If we expect another person to react in a certain way to a given situation, and they fail to meet our expectation, do I have the right to be disappointed or angry? It's good to have high standards, but only if we're prepared to accept disappointing results.

- When we let go of expectations we won't feel resentful. If we can adjust our expectations we'll no longer set ourselves up for constant disappointment.

- Celebrate every accomplishment, no matter how small, and be grateful for it.

What is the Answer?

Ask a volunteer to read the paragraph. Ask for comments. Then ask, "What does it look like to 'relax into acceptance'? How do we do that? What are realistic expectations?

We'll find peace of mind when we stop expecting and relax into acceptance. Contentment comes from accepting gratefully the good that comes to us, not from raging at life because it's not better. And don't take it personally when you're disappointed. This is by no means resignation, but a realistic acceptance of how things are.

What We Need To Remember

Ask volunteers to read each statement. Encourage discussion. Then ask, "Which statement(s) stands out to you?"

- We are powerless over _____.

- We cannot change our child, but God can!

- Control is an illusion. We have none. But God is in control!

- Stop expecting (at least lower expectations) and accept what is.

- Becoming more informed about our child's issues (bi-polar, self harm, pornography, alcoholism, etc.) will also help us know what is realistic to expect.

- Accept gratefully any good that comes to us.

- I, too, often fail to live up to the expectations of others.

- Be thankful for the smallest things.

- The Serenity Prayer can lead us to contentment.

Scripture

Lead the group to read these two scripture passages in unison. Say, "Let's read these scripture verses out loud together."

Philippians 4:12
"I have learned to be content in any and every situation."

Romans 15:7 NLT
"Therefore, accept each other, just as Christ has accepted you so that God will be given glory."

Reflection

Ask, *"What do you need to remember most from this session?"*

Prayer

NOTES

Session 11

GUARDING YOUR MARRIAGE

GUARDING YOUR MARRIAGE

Session Aim:

To motivate parents to protect their marriage especially during a crisis.

Key Principles:

Crisis in any form can put a marriage relationship at risk. Many parents fall into the routine of daily combat, which eventually leads to a parting of the ways. Guarding your marriage relationship can divide the hardships and double your joy.

Scripture:

Ecclesiastes 4:9–10

"Two are better than one, because they have a good return for their labor: If either of them falls down, one can help the other up. But pity anyone who falls and has no one to help them up."

1 Corinthians 13:4–8

"Love is patient, love is kind. It does not envy, it does not boast, it is not proud. It does not dishonor others, it is not self-seeking, it is not easily angered, it keeps no record of wrongs. Love does not delight in evil but rejoices with the truth. It always protects, always trusts, and always hopes, always perseveres. Love never fails."

Resources:

Parents with Broken Hearts by William Coleman, chapter 14

Don't Let Your Kids Kill You by Charles Rubin, chapter 1

Hit by a Ton of Bricks by John Vawter, chapter 7

Loving a Prodigal by H. Norman Wright, Chapter 5

Session: GUARDING YOUR MARRIAGE

Family Issues

* Some participants may be single parents. Explain that this session is about marriage and may not apply specifically to them. However, there is still helpful content for their benefit.

* Delay having participants open their books until after you've asked the question under the section: What Can We Do to Guard Our Marriage in Times of Crisis?

Introduction

Ask, *"On a scale of 1–10, 1 being low and 10 being high, what is your stress level with your child right now and why?"*

Read *this statement to the group.*

"Crisis in any form can put a marriage relationship at risk. Many parents fall into the routine of daily combat, which eventually leads to a parting of the ways."

Ask, *"What problems do you think having a rebellious child can cause in a marriage?"* *Allow* *time for answers.*

Possible Answers:

After discussion, share any points not mentioned.

- Added stress in their lives
- Strain and tension in relationships
- More arguing, disagreements, and conflict
- Increased irritability
- Misunderstanding—male/female differences as well as temperament differences
- Being too consumed by the problem—talking about it all the time
- Overlooked or decreased time for each other
- Blame and criticize one another
- Lack of unity—not being on the same page
- Withdraw from each other—isolation

What Can We Do to Guard Our Marriage in Times of Crisis?

Ask, *"What have you done to guard your marriage when you went through a crisis?" Encourage sharing.*

Tell the group to turn to this session in their Parent Notebook. Ask volunteers to take turns reading the list. Discuss what stands out to them.

- Make time for fun, plan a date night once a week and declare it a "no prodigal zone."

- Take turns being the bad guy.

- Present a united front—never disagree in front of a rebellious child. Resolve differences privately.

- Make your marriage your number one priority, not your child—one day your child will move on and you will be left with each other.

- Memorize and practice these statements: "You may be right" (defuses arguments). "What do you need from me right now?" "I'm not the enemy" (keeps perspective).

- Stop blaming and criticizing each other.

- Forgive mistakes and failures.

- The word divorce is not in your vocabulary. Refuse to consider it as an option.

- Pray together. When needed, agree to allow time for emotions to subside before praying.

- Accept that neither of you were perfect parents.

- Be a good listener, slow to speak, not quick to fix.

- Cultivate a hobby together.

- Be honest and vulnerable with your feelings.

- Be grateful for the calm times.

- Intentionally involve yourselves in marriage-building activities (conferences, seminars, small group studies, reading books together, counseling, etc.).

Scripture and Activity

Ask volunteers to read the following scriptures.

Ecclesiastes 4:9–10

"Two are better than one, because they have a good return for their labor: If either of them falls down, one can help the other up. But pity anyone who falls and has no one to help them up."

1 Corinthians 13:4–8

"Love is patient, love is kind. It does not envy, it does not boast, it is not proud. It does not dishonor others, it is not self-seeking, it is not easily angered, it keeps no record of wrongs. Love does not delight in evil but rejoices with the truth. It always protects, always trusts, and always hopes, always perseveres. Love never fails."

Say, *"As couples, privately discuss what new guarding activities you want to start doing."* *Suggest they conclude their time in prayer.*

*If someone came without their spouse or is a single parent, suggest they get together for prayer with other single parents or with you, the facilitator.

Prayer

Depending on the time you may want to delete this part since people just finished praying together.

NOTES

Session 12

GUARDING YOUR FAMILY

GUARDING YOUR FAMILY

Session Aim:

To motivate parents to protect the relationships with their other children, especially during crisis.

Key Principles:

Crisis in any form can put family relationships at risk. Many parents fall into the trap of being preoccupied with their troubled child so much that other children can be neglected. The troubled child can negatively impact other siblings.

Scripture:

Luke 15:22–32

Parable of the Lost Son

"But the father said to his servants, 'Quick! Bring the best robe and put it on him. Put a ring on his finger and sandals on his feet. Bring the fattened calf and kill it. Let's have a feast and celebrate. For this son of mine was dead and is alive again; he was lost and is found.' So they began to celebrate. Meanwhile, the older son was in the field. When he came near the house, he heard music and dancing. So he called one of the servants and asked what was going on. 'Your brother has come,' he replied, 'and your father has killed the fattened calf because he has him back safe and sound.' "

"The older brother became angry and refused to go in. So his father went out and pleaded with him. But he answered his father, 'Look! All these years I've been slaving for you and never disobeyed your orders. Yet you never gave me even a young goat so that I could celebrate with my friends. But when this son of yours who has squandered your property with prostitutes comes home, you kill the fattened calf for him!'

" 'My son,' the father said, 'you are always with me, and everything I have is yours. But we had to celebrate and be glad, because this brother of yours was dead and is alive; he was lost and is found.' "

Ephesians 6:4

"Fathers, do not exasperate your children; instead, bring them up in the training and instruction of the Lord."

Resources:

Loving a Prodigal by H. Normal Wright, chapter 5

Session: GUARDING YOUR FAMILY

*Some parents may only have one child, their prodigal, so this session may not apply to them. They can support others in the group and gain information.

Introduction

Ask, *"Were you an only child or did you have other siblings? If you had other siblings, where were you in the birth order? Did you have a sibling who had troubles? How has that affected you?"*

Trouble with Our Other Children

Read, *"Crisis in any form can add stress to family relationships. If we have other children, they can be negatively affected by having a troubled brother or sister. This is our topic for today."*

Ask *the questions and encourage discussion. If any content below doesn't come up from the group ask volunteers to read the list.*

What are some problems that can arise with our other children?

- Resentment, anger, and jealousy can build up.

- We give so much time and attention to our troubled child it takes away from them.

- Financial resources the family might have enjoyed are spent on the rebelling child.

- Vacations, education limitations, extracurricular activities or sports, etc. may make siblings feel cheated because of how their sibling affected these.

- Anger at how they saw us be hurt by their brother or sister—they tire of their behavior and don't like it. They can become like the older brother in the parable of the prodigal son.

- Depression, sadness, or worry over their sibling's welfare—they may need counseling.

- Caretaking—they begin to feel responsible for their sibling; try to protect or keep secrets to keep them safe or maintain peace in the family.

How does this make you feel?

In what ways has enabling negatively impacted other children in your family?

What have you done to prevent or remedy these problems?

Suggestions

Ask volunteers to read the list and discuss.

- Intentionally spend time with your other children doing normal, meaningful, and fun things together.

- If they no longer live with you, call, email, text, or Skype to stay connected.

- Make extra effort to give your other children lots of positive affirmation. Praise them and compliment them as much as possible for their strengths and the blessing they are to you.

- Make time to do special things with and for your other children. Save to give them a special surprise or vacation of their choosing.

- If possible, arrange a family counseling time. Give opportunities for them to express their feelings; family sessions can be therapeutic and healing.

Scripture

Ask for two volunteers to read the scripture passages.

Luke 15:22–32

Parable of the Lost Son

"But the father said to his servants, 'Quick! Bring the best robe and put it on him. Put a ring on his finger and sandals on his feet. Bring the fattened calf and kill it. Let's have a feast and celebrate. For this son of mine was dead and is alive again; he was lost and is found.' So they began to celebrate. Meanwhile, the older son was in the field. When he came near the house, he heard music and dancing. So he called one of the servants and asked what was going on. 'Your brother has come,' he replied, 'and your father has killed the fattened calf because he has him back safe and sound.'

The older brother became angry and refused to go in. So his father went out and pleaded with him. But he answered his father, 'Look! All these years I've been slaving for you and never disobeyed your orders. Yet you never gave me even a young goat so that I could celebrate with my friends. But when this son of yours who has squandered your property with prostitutes comes home, you kill the fattened calf for him!'

'My son,' the father said, 'you are always with me, and everything I have is yours. But we had to celebrate and be glad, because this brother of yours was dead and is alive; he was lost and is found.' "

Ephesians 6:4
"Fathers, do not exasperate your children; instead, bring them up in the training and instruction of the Lord."

Reflection

Ask, "What is your take away from this session?"

Prayer

NOTES

Session 13

POWERLESSNESS
AND
CONTROL

POWERLESSNESS AND CONTROL

Session Aim:

To admit we are powerless to change or control our rebellious children.

Key Principles:

We didn't cause our child's destructive choices. We can't cure them and we can't control them. When our children were younger we had some control. Once they are adults, control is an illusion.

Scripture:

Philippians 2:13
"For it is God who works in you to will and to act in order to fulfill his good purpose."

Philippians 1:6
"Being confident of this, that he who began a good work in you will carry it on to completion until the day of Christ Jesus."

Resources:

Al-Anon slogans

Declaration of Release[2]

Setting Boundaries with Your Adult Children by Allison Bottke

Session: POWERLESSNESS

Introduction

Ask these three questions and allow time for responses.

"What do you have control over in your life?"

"How do you respond to having no control?"

"How does that make you feel?"

Three Concepts

Have participants turn to their notebooks. Ask a volunteer to read the Three Concepts and then discuss each one. This is a revised Al-Anon slogan.

I am not the cause of my child's problems.

Ultimately, I can't control my child's problems.

I don't have the power to fix my child's problems.

Ask volunteers to read the following paragraphs. Encourage comments and discussion.

- It's not your fault, unless you encouraged your child's behavior and aided in their destruction. Stop trying to control. You'll drive yourself crazy and them too. You can't fix them—they have to want to change. You can't force it. Remember, control is an illusion. The only thing we really have control over is ourselves. There's nothing you can do to speed up the healing process, but God is still in control.

- As parents, we seek help as a last resort. We find it difficult to surrender to the idea that we, who are usually competent, don't really know how to handle this correctly. Our natural impulse is to take over. This only causes trouble. We have to let go and let God.

- If we really accept the fact that we have no authority or power over another person, then we will not try to force them to do what we want them to do. Admitting our powerlessness is by no means a statement of despair. It helps us accept our limitations and keeps us humble, so that we can find answers that will place our lives on a different course. It prepares us for deliverance from problems we can't cope with alone.

Declaration of Release

Direct group members to take five to ten minutes on their own to read the Declaration of Release and then use it as their own prayer for their child. (The Declaration of Release is found in the appendix of their Parent Notebook.)

Reflection

Ask, "What is your take-away from this session?"

Prayer

DECLARATION OF RELEASE

Make this declaration of release[2] as often as necessary:

Because Jesus Christ is my Lord, I free you from my anxiety, fears, and control. I trust the Holy Spirit to lead you and show you the way that is right for you—the way of love, joy, and peace and all that salvation includes.

I place you at God's throne of grace. I cannot force my will on you. I cannot live your life for you. I give you to God the Father, Son, and Holy Spirit. You are a very special person. As much as I love you, God loves you more. Your life today is totally in His hands, and I trust Him with it.

In Jesus' name

I release you from my expectations,

I place you on open palms to the Lord,

I give you my blessings,

I let you go.

In His love,

Signed_____

Date _____

"It is God who works in you to will and to act according to his good purpose; being confident of this, that he who began a good work in you will carry it on to completion until the day of Christ Jesus" (Philippians 2:13, 1:6).

[2] Used with permission from @Sylvia Gunter, The Father's Business, P. O. Box 380333, Birmingham, AL 35238 www.thefathersbusiness.com. Email: info@thefathersbusiness.com

NOTES

Session 14

COMMUNICATION

COMMUNICATION

Session Aim:

To understand the purpose of communication, the qualities of good talkers and listeners, and why people are not good at each, and to learn techniques for good communication.

Key Principles:

Communication always has two roles. Techniques can be learned for good communication.

Scripture:

James 1:19

"My dear brothers and sisters, take note of this: Everyone should be quick to listen, slow to speak and slow to become angry."

Ephesians 4:15 NLT

"Instead, we will speak the truth in love, growing in every way more and more like Christ, who is the head of his body, the church."

Resources:

Cumberland Heights Family Program: www.cumberlandheights.org

Session: COMMUNICATION

Introduction

Ask, *"What is the purpose of communication?" Encourage responses.*

After discussion have a volunteer read these three points:

To share information

To express needs

To get to know others better

Two Roles of Communication

Read, "In communication there are always two roles: the talker and the listener."

What Are the Qualities of a Good Talker and a Good Listener?

Ask two volunteers to read the qualities of a good talker and listener. One is the talker and the other is the listener, alternating one line at a time (i.e. talker reads: "Look at the listener" then listener reads: "Look at the talker").

TALKER	LISTENER
Look at the listener	Look at the talker
Speak loudly enough	Do not interrupt
Speak clearly	Ask questions
Use more than one tone of voice	Repeat back what you hear
Don't go on and on	Look interested
Think about what you want to say	Care about what the talker is saying
Use words the listener will understand	Don't talk when the talker is sharing

Ask, "Where do you see your strengths and weaknesses?"

Why are people not good listeners or talkers?

Ask volunteers to read the reasons.

TALKER	LISTENER
Fear	Anger
Shy	Bored
Have nothing to say	Tired
As a child learned not to talk	Too Busy

Uncertain how to express thoughts   Distracted

                                                 Cannot hear

                                                 Under influence

Techniques for Good Communication

Ask volunteers to read. Encourage discussion.

- Give your undivided attention – stop what you're doing, set another time to talk, and respect the time set to talk.

- Take your time—speak slowly, breathe, plan ahead, and sit down.

- Use "I" messages: "I feel _____ when you _____ because _____". This is a good model.

- Speak respectfully—avoid name-calling, yelling, or cursing.

- Allow everyone to have their own feelings, regardless of what they are.

- Verbally recognize both of your feelings and those of the other person – we feel better knowing someone recognizes how we feel, even if they do not agree with us. Heart feelings such as: mad, sad, glad and scared.

- Listen to the person speaking—don't think about what your response will be, and say back what you think you have heard.

- Ask for what you want—don't make demands.

- Remember to show appreciation to the person for their time and effort—don't take this time for granted especially with family members and close friends.

Reflection

Ask, "Which techniques would you like to apply to your communication skills?"

Refer to the Communication Worksheet in the parent notebook. Encourage parents to plan a time to do this activity with their children to improve communication.

Scriptures

James 1:19

"My dear brothers and sisters, take note of this: Everyone should be quick to listen, slow to speak and slow to become angry."

Ephesians 4:15 NLT

"Instead, we will speak the truth in love, growing in every way more and more like Christ, who is the head of his body, the church."

Prayer

COMMUNICATION WORKSHEET

Learning healthy communication is vital. Complete this form stating positive and negative to the person you will be communicating with, using honesty and feeling words.

1. I feel/felt _____ and _____
    when _____.

2. I feel/felt _____ and _____
    when _____.

3. I feel/felt _____ and _____
    when _____.

4. I feel/felt _____ and _____
    when _____.

5. I feel/felt _____ and _____
    when _____.

6. I feel/felt _____ and _____
    when _____.

7. I feel/felt _____ and _____
    when _____.

8. I feel/felt _____ and _____
    when _____.

9. I feel/felt _____ and _____
    when _____.

10. I feel/felt _____ and _____
    when _____.

NOTES

Session 15

WAITING

WAITING

Session Aim:

To acknowledge the waiting times in our lives and recognize our struggle with waiting while learning there are benefits to its practice.

Key Principles:

Life is full of waiting. How we wait is important. Waiting well develops godly qualities.

Scripture:

Psalm 27:14

"Wait for the LORD; be strong and take heart and wait for the Lord."

Psalm 130:5

"I wait for the LORD; my whole being waits, and in his word I put my hope."

Psalm 37:7

"Be still before the LORD; . . . wait patiently for him; . . . do not fret."

Romans 8:25

"But if we hope for what we do not yet have, we wait for it patiently."

Resources:

The Hope of a Homecoming, O'Rourke and Sauer, chapter 11

Wild Child, Waiting Mom by Karilee Hayden and Wendi Hayden English

The Hurting Parent by Margie M. Lewis and Gregg Lewis

Session: WAITING

Introduction

Read the definition of waiting.

Definition

"Waiting: to remain inactive or in a state of repose, as until something expected happens; to look forward to eagerly" (www.dictionary.com).

Ask, "What are times in our lives when we have to wait?"

Possible responses are: in a doctor's office; at a traffic light; in line at a store or event; being on hold on the phone; life events such as graduation, marriage, having children, getting a job, Christ's return, etc.

Looking Deeper at Waiting

Ask the following questions and allow time for group responses.

"What are you waiting for regarding your child?"

"Why is it hard for us to wait for these things in our child's life?"

Possible responses to the second question: the seriousness of their circumstances, we're not in control, it feels like inactivity, fear of the unknown or uncertainty of the outcome.

Ask a volunteer to read the paragraph below:

Waiting is hard work. It takes a lot of concentrated effort and a special kind of self-discipline. Today, waiting goes against everything our culture emphasizes. The problem is, "it took time for our children to get themselves into trouble, and getting . . . out of trouble will probably take time as well."[3]

Ask, "How does this make you feel?"

Possible responses: inadequate, stressed, depressed, on edge, anxious, angry, resentful, restless, hopeless, impatient, dreading the phone to ring, afraid for their welfare.

Consequences of Not Waiting

Ask, "What are some of the consequences you can think of that come from not waiting or not waiting well?"

Waiting Well

Ask a volunteer to read the paragraph and the scriptures.

Waiting is often part of life and our spiritual life is no different. God places us in positions to wait on Him and asks us to do it with patience and expectation of His work in our lives. It helps us focus on who is ultimately in control. We grow in our faith and trust in God. It's okay to tell Him you're exhausted and don't like it. It gives opportunities to develop patience.

Scriptures

Psalm 27:14

"Wait for the LORD; be strong and take heart and wait for the Lord."

Psalm 130:5

"I wait for the LORD; my whole being waits, and in his word I put my hope."

Psalm 37:7

"Be still before the LORD; . . . wait patiently for him; . . . do not fret."

Romans 8:25

"But if we hope for what we do not yet have, we wait for it patiently."

Tips for Waiting Well

Ask, "What helps you wait?" After discussion, ask volunteers to read the tips.

- Being more focused on God.
- Remember who God is and what He can do.
- Continue to live your life, be active with work, friends, community, etc.
- Take one day at a time; live in the present.
- Remember the promises of God.
- Get someone else's perspective.
- Keep the big picture in mind. God is developing something in us.

- Remind yourself of God's goodness.

Ask, *"Can you add to this list?"*

Reflection

Ask, *"What stood out to you most from this session?"*

Prayer

[3] Brendan O'Rourke and DeEtte Sauer, *The Hope of a Homecoming* (Colorado Springs: NavPress, 2003), 117.

NOTES

Session 16

SURVIVING THE HOLIDAYS

SURVIVING THE HOLIDAYS

Session Aim:

To help parents go through a holiday with less pain and frustration.

Key Principles:

Holidays are special times that are often accompanied with expectations, traditions, celebrations and memories. However, when parents are hurting over the destructive choices of their children, these days can bring an increased sense of loss, anger, and pain. There are actions they can take that will help them survive the holidays in better emotional shape and possibly find new meaning and enjoyment.

Scripture:

Matthew 6:10
"Your kingdom come, your will be done."

Ephesians 4:32 NASB
"Be kind to one another, tender-hearted, forgiving each other, just as God in Christ also has forgiven you."

Isaiah 43:18–19
"Forget the former things; do not dwell on the past. See, I am doing a new thing!"

Philippians 2:4 NASB
"Do not merely look out for your own personal interests, but also for the interests of others."

1 Thessalonians 5:18
"Give thanks in all circumstances; for this is God's will for you in Christ Jesus."

Resources:

Al-Anon literature

Materials Needed:

If you can afford it, purchase one small notepad for each person in the group to record their gratitude list. See tip #4. (Notepads are inexpensive at a Dollar Store.)

Session: Surviving the Holidays

Introduction

Say, *"Holidays can be a time of celebration with family and friends. However, when we are hurting over the destructive choices of our children, holidays can be a time of increased pain and sadness. They can be reminders of special days in the past we greatly enjoyed with them and bring to the surface feelings of sadness, loss, and grief instead of joy, gratitude, and celebration. Let's look at a few tips for surviving the holidays."*

Tips for Surviving the Holidays

Ask, *"What are some expectations you may have of your child for this holiday? Pause and let the group answer. Have volunteers* ***read*** *each tip and discuss them one at a time."*

Tip # 1: Adjust or lower your expectations.

Sometimes we don't realize the expectations we have until they go unfulfilled. Feelings of disappointment, frustration, hurt, anger, and resentment alert us that we had an expectation our child did not meet.

"Expectations are premeditated resentments," according to Al-Anon. When we hold an expectation that isn't met, we feel disappointed and hurt. Disappointment and hurt can turn into anger. Anger, over time, can result in resentment.

If you can adjust your expectations it will protect your fragile emotions. You can avoid becoming disappointed, hurt, angry, or resentful. Let go of how you wish things would be. Have no expectations of your child's participation or involvement. Then, if things work out the way you wanted, great! You'll be pleasantly surprised.

Matthew 6:10
"Your kingdom come, your will be done."

Ephesians 4:32

"Be kind to one another, tender-hearted, forgiving each other, just as God in Christ also has forgiven you."

Tip #2: Consider doing things differently this year.

Relevant to the upcoming holiday, what are some traditions that are special to you?

Maybe your former traditions will make you feel worse or be too difficult to do in light of your situation with your son or daughter. If you always cooked a big meal, you could go to a restaurant or to someone else's house instead. If you opened gifts at night, then change it up and open them in the morning.

Isaiah 43:18–19

"Forget the former things; do not dwell on the past. See, I am doing a new thing!"

Tip #3: Focus on others.

Look for a way to help someone else who has a need. Do something kind for them. You don't have to look too far to find hurting or lonely people. It could be as simple as sending them a card, visiting, or calling them. You could take them out for coffee or a meal; give a box of candy, flowers, or a gift card. Be creative. Mow a lawn, pick up some groceries, or fix something around the house. Focusing on someone else takes your attention off yourself and lightens the burden you are carrying. Doing it anonymously would be extra fun.

Philippians 2:4 NASB

"Do not merely look out for your own personal interests, but also for the interests of others."

Tip #4: Be grateful.

Keep giving thanks no matter how you feel. Start a thanksgiving journal or a gratitude list. Write down at least one thing in it every day. Don't include only big things: a job, a promotion at work, a new car, etc. Notice little things too—birds singing, the wonder and beauty of nature, a smell of something you like (food cooking on a grill, flowers), friendship, eating something delicious, etc.

What are you grateful for right now?

1 Thessalonians 5:18

"Always giving thanks to God the Father for everything, in the name of our Lord Jesus Christ."

Give *each participant a notepad to record their gratitude list. Encourage them to write down one thing they are grateful for right now.*

Conclusion

Say, *"If you try any of these things it will help you survive the holidays in better emotional shape than if you didn't. Try at least one of these ideas. If it helps you, then share about it with a friend. You never know; they may need a few survival tips themselves!"*

Reflection

Ask, "Which tips have you done before? Which are you willing to try?"

Prayer

NOTES

Session 17

COURAGEOUS LOVE

COURAGEOUS LOVE

Session Aim:

Parents will explore what courageous love looks like and gain new ideas on how they can show it to their challenging children. This love demonstrates how parents can face a crisis, take a stand, meet challenges, and continue loving their wayward sons and daughters. Courageous love will help them develop new strengths so they can stay connected and support their children with healthy boundaries.

Key Principles:

Courageous love is love that doesn't enable or over-help. God's love for us is our example and motivation.

Scripture:

Romans 5:8 ESV

"God shows his love for us in that while we were still sinners, Christ died for us."

1 Corinthians 13:4–8 ESV

"Love is patient and kind; love does not envy or boast; it is not arrogant or rude. It does not insist on its own way; it is not irritable or resentful; it does not rejoice at wrongdoing, but rejoices with the truth. Love bears all things, believes all things, hopes all things, endures all things. Love never ends."

Psalm 118:1

"Give thanks to the LORD, for he is good; his love endures forever."

Resources:

Relief for Hurting Parents by Buddy Scott, chapter 9

Co-parenting with God by Peter Lord, chapters 9–11

Tough Love by Phyllis and David York and Ted Wachtel

Codependent No More by Melody Beattie, chapter 11

How Al-Anon Works: For Families and Friends of Alcoholics, Al-Anon Family Group Literature, chapter 11

Mom I Hate My Life! by Sharon A. Hersh

Materials Needed:

Make two signs. You can use 8 ½ x 11 printer paper. On one, print "Agree" and on the other print "Disagree." You'll need some way of putting them on the walls on either side of the room you meet in. Do this before beginning the meeting.

Session: COURAGEOUS LOVE

Introduction

Say, *"Today we're going to talk about love, courageous love. This is love that doesn't enable or over help. We're going to discuss what it looks like and see if we can gain any new ideas on how we can show this kind of love to our challenging sons and daughters."*

Ask *a volunteer to read the following statement:*

Courageous love teaches us to face the crisis, take a stand, and meet challenges. This type of love will help us develop new strengths so we can give a sense of direction and support.

Agree or Disagree?

Say, *"I'm going to read some statements. Decide if you agree or disagree. On one side of the room is a sign that says Agree, on the other is Disagree. After I read the statement, stand on the side that shows your opinion. Do you have any questions?"* (*This list is in their notebooks.*)

1. Love means never having to say you're sorry.

2. I will always bail my son out of jail.

3. I have to tell my daughter (who's over 18) to move out of my home for not living by my rules. It's the most loving thing I can do.

4. I refuse to call in sick for my son when he can't get up and go to work due to a hangover or staying out too late.

5. It's showing love to step in and make sure they don't fail a class or lose their job.

6. Because we love our child, we took out a second mortgage on our home to pay for their fourth rehab. It's the right thing to do to show them we believe in them.

7. I refuse to drain my savings account or retirement plan to pay my daughter's bills. I'll let her experience the consequences.

8. I will write an excuse for my son's absence from school, even though he didn't have a valid reason.

9. I covered my child with a blanket on the front lawn when they passed out drunk. I left them there. I didn't drag them into the house or put them to bed.

10. I forgave a debt my daughter owed me because I knew she could never pay me back.

11. I will pay for my child's cell phone so I can have contact with them.

12. After my child moves out, I will buy them a meal once a month (or have them over for one), but I won't give them any money or gift cards.

13. I keep telling my son what he should do. If I don't, he'll forget.

14. I refuse to have a relationship with my gay child's partner. It goes against my beliefs.

Tell the group to sit down and turn to this session in their notebook. Ask, "Did you have any new insights during this activity? Which of the statements I read don't feel loving to you?"

Courageous Love

Say, "Here are some suggestions on how to show courageous love."

Ask volunteers to read each statement. Guide discussion.

Show them Christ. He is what they really need above all else. It's not an excuse to nag or preach. This often has the opposite effect. Our behavior and attitudes can speak more than words. Christ is our motivation to continue loving them even when they don't deserve it.

Pray. Only God can change them. Ask others to be part of a prayer team to pray for them and their friends. Email specific requests each week—be sure to include how they can pray for you. Prayer is a powerful way to show our love.

Tell them. Even when our children are rebellious, they need to hear that we still love them and see our love in action. When things are at their worst, we're still called to love. When we reach out we might be rejected, but we can't stop. Speak it, text it, email it; do all you can to stay connected. However, don't let them trample on you or not pay the consequences for their destructive choices. Love is not a doormat.

Keep a journal. If you don't know where they are or have no way of communicating, you could start keeping a journal. Record things you and the family are doing, things you think would be of interest to them. It could be daily or weekly. Include an expression of love to them with each entry. When they come "home," give them the journal. It might open the door to help rebuild your relationship.

Welcome them home. Let them know when they're ready to change, your door is always open. You'll be there with open arms to help, encourage, and support them. But don't create too many requirements for returning that could lessen the chances of them coming home.

Listen. Another powerful way of showing love is by simply listening. Look for opportunities to just sit with them (maybe on the phone) and listen. Even if they're drunk or high, being there speaks volumes: "Tell me more about that. Tell me what you're feeling. I love you. I care." Be persistent. Don't give up. Once they realize how much you care, it can make all the difference.

Respect their friends. Even if you don't like their friends, be kind, thoughtful, and courteous the way you would to any unbeliever. Remember, their friends are someone else's wayward children too. Your son or daughter will take notice of this. You never know the affect it may have later on.

Take an interest in what they like. Learn about it so you can ask good questions. Validate those things. Encourage them in these pursuits.

Be strong. When you have to correct or discipline (under age 18) always end with, "We love you too much not to do anything about this."

When asked for money or help that would be enabling, say, "Because we love you, we're not going to step in and take away your privilege of figuring this out on your own. We're confident you can do it and we'll pray for you." Instead, invite them over for a meal or meet at a restaurant, or a coffee shop.

When they've failed in some way, experienced something traumatic, or relapsed, say, "There's nothing you could ever do—or could be done to you—that would ever make me love you any less or any more than I always have. My love for you will never change."

Keep boundaries. Love needs healthy boundaries to thrive and protect both parties. Neither should take advantage of the other, nor do anything that's not in the best interest of each person. Sometimes the loving thing to do is the hardest thing to do.

Ask, "How can we love without enabling our troubled children?"

A True Story

Read or ask a volunteer the true story below.

When one couple's son was incarcerated in a state prison for six years, the immediate and extended family (including close friends) agreed to take turns accepting a weekly collect phone call from him so they could stay connected and let him know they still cared. His parents visited weekly and when they couldn't go, another family member or friend went in their place. They gave him clear ultimatums and accepted no excuses. They were willing to go so far, but he had to do his part. They let him know, in no uncertain terms, that they would support him and help him this one time and that would be it. He knew they meant what they said. When he got out of prison, he had a better understanding of their love for him, and how far they were willing to go in order to show it. But he also better understood the boundaries they were s etting within that love. Today, twenty years later, he says their courageous love made the difference and changed the course of his life.

Reflection

Ask, "What do you want to do differently? How will you try to show love to your child this week?"

Scripture

Read these verses out loud together before you pray.

Romans 5:8 ESV
"God shows his love for us in that while we were still sinners, Christ died for us."

1 Corinthians 13:4–8 ESV

"Love is patient and kind; love does not envy or boast; it is not arrogant or rude. It does not insist on its own way; it is not irritable or resentful; it does not rejoice at wrongdoing, but rejoices with the truth. Love bears all things, believes all things, hopes all things, endures all things. Love never ends."

Psalm 118:1

"Give thanks to the LORD;, for he is good; his love endures forever."

Ask, *"What stood out most to you in this session?"*

Prayer

NOTES

Session 18

FORGIVENESS

FORGIVENESS

Session Aim:

Parents will recognize the value of forgiveness in five areas and make progress in their own journey.

Key Principles:

Forgiveness benefits the forgiver. Without it we remain stuck in our recovery journey. Forgiveness doesn't make the other person right; it makes us free.

Scripture:

Ephesians 4:32

"Be kind and compassionate to one another, forgiving each other, just as in Christ God forgave you."

Luke 6:37

"Forgive, and you will be forgiven."

Colossians 3:13

"Bear with each other and forgive one another if any of you has a grievance against someone. Forgive as the Lord forgave you."

Resources:

Setting Boundaries with Your Adult Children by Allison Bottke, chapter 5

Addict in the Family by Beverly Conyers, chapter 7

Parents with Broken Hearts by William Coleman, chapter 12

Session: FORGIVENESS

Introduction

Say, _"In today's session we are going to discuss forgiveness. We'll look at what it is and five areas where it may be needed. Then we'll explore the consequences of not forgiving."_

Definition

Ask, _"How do you define forgiveness?" Wait for their answers._ **_Ask_** _someone to read the three bullet points and then discuss. Follow this pattern for each section of this session._

- Forgiveness is not just for the person who needs to be forgiven. It also benefits us, the "forgiver."
- Forgiveness doesn't make the other person right; it makes you free. (Al-Anon)
- Forgiveness isn't condoning or excusing the actions or behaviors of others. It's releasing that person to God to let Him deal with them, so we can be set free. For parents in pain, it's part of the process of gaining back our lives.

Some of our children don't even remember or know they need forgiving. Therefore, one reason to forgive is for our own sake and for our own health.

"If we hold on to our anger, we stop growing and our souls begin to shrivel." — M. Scott Peck

Our child may have made decisions and choices that hurt us and cost us a lot: loss of health, sleep, time at work, or finances spent trying to help them or ourselves; loss of or damaged relationships—with them, our spouse, other children, other family members and even friends; loss of our mental and emotional well-being. Our faith can be weakened; we may even walk away from God in disappointment and confusion.

Five Areas of Forgiveness

1. Forgive our child—for hurting us. We may feel very angry and resentful over how we've been treated. They lied to us, stole from us; told us they hated us, we ruined their lives, and they wanted to get away from us. They broke our hearts and shattered our dreams. We don't trust them, can't believe them, don't even know them anymore. We also feel angry at what they're doing to themselves. The list goes on and on. We must forgive, even if they don't ask us to. Jesus said, "Forgive and you will be forgiven" (Luke 6:37).

2. Forgive ourselves—for not being the perfect parent. There isn't one. Even though we did our best, we still tend to feel a lot of guilt over any part we may have played. Be easy on yourself. Refuse the lie that it's your fault. You didn't make them do any of this. You did the best you could. No matter how badly you may have blown it, it doesn't excuse their choices.

   If we don't forgive ourselves, we'll end up living under the weight of guilt, blame, shame, and a host of other feelings that God never intended. He gave our children a free will to make their own decisions. Don't forget what happened in the Garden of Eden to the only perfect parent (Genesis 2).

3. Forgive others—for hurting our child. This includes those who influenced them negatively, encouraged their destructive choices, sold or gave them drugs, exposed them to pornography, took advantage of them, or didn't help them when they could have. Our friends may hurt us or walk away. They can't handle our pain. They want to, but they can't. It's not their fault. They can't understand what we're going through.

4. Forgive God—sounds strange, doesn't it? It can be very difficult to accept that while God is sovereign and all-powerful, and could have prevented these things, He gave them free will to choose for themselves. Sometimes we blame Him for not protecting them, even though they simply experienced the natural consequences of their choices. Of course He doesn't need to be forgiven. He didn't do anything wrong. In reality, we may need to be forgiven if we've begun to blame Him, allowing resentment to build up in our hearts— maybe without even realizing it. The important thing is to be honest. Tell Him what we're feeling, even if we're angry. It's okay. He understands.

5. Ask forgiveness from our adult children—for mistakes we made. We may or may not have known God and His ways in the years we were raising them. Most of us made at least a few mistakes. Asking their forgiveness brings relief and healing. If God reveals a time when we unintentionally hurt our child—too harsh, too lenient, or enabled—asking forgiveness can have huge benefits for our relationship. Allison Bottke says, "Though very hard, (it) may be the healing balm needed to prepare them for a spiritual growth spurt. Then again, it could be like pouring lighter fluid on an open flame. You don't know until you try."[4]

Louise Smedes said it so well: "The first and only person to be healed by forgiveness is the person who does the forgiveness. . . . When we genuinely forgive, we set a prisoner free and then discover that the prisoner we set free was us."

Consequences of Not Forgiving

Ask, *"What do you think will happen if we don't forgive?" Encourage comments.*

Ask *a volunteer to read the following paragraph and scripture verse. All are in their notebook.*

We need to offer and receive forgiveness. If we don't, it will lead to bitterness, resentment, and cynicism. It's the only way to lance the wounds of our heart before they begin to fester and make us sick. Jesus is our role model. We forgive out of obedience to Him because He forgave us. He is the how and the why of forgiving. Forgiveness is a long, slow process, but if we choose to do it, we can be set free.

Ephesians 4:32
"Be kind and compassionate to one another, forgiving each other, just as in Christ God forgave you."

Reflection

Ask, *"What is your take-away from this section?"*

Prayer

[4] Allison Bottke, *Setting Boundaries with Your Adult Children* (Eugene, OR: Harvest House, 2008), chapter 5

NOTES

Session 19

THANKFULNESS

THANKFULLNESS

Session Aim:

To help parents realize that even though they don't feel like it, being thankful in the midst of their trials can refocus their attention on positive things, lighten their burdens, and increase their awareness of God's activity in their lives.

Key Principles:

The Bible teaches us to be thankful in all circumstances. This is God's will. But it's very difficult to do when we're going through painful experiences. Gratitude in painful situations requires dependence on God and practice.

Scripture:

1 Thessalonians 5:18 ESV
"Give thanks in all circumstances; for this is the will of God in Christ Jesus for you."

Ephesians 5:20
"Always giving thanks to God the Father for everything, in the name of our Lord Jesus Christ."

Philippians 4:6–7
"Do not be anxious about anything, but in every situation, by prayer and petition, with thanksgiving, present your requests to God. And the peace of God, which transcends all understanding, will guard your hearts and your minds in Christ Jesus."

Materials Needed:

A sheet of paper for each parent (printer paper is fine).

A small notepad for each person. (These can be purchased at a Dollar Store.)

Arrange to play relaxing, wordless music during the activity, if it's possible for your setting.

Resources:

One Thousand Gifts by Ann Voskamp

Highlights from the Research Project on Gratitude and Thankfulness: Dimensions and Perspectives of Gratitude, Co-Investigators: Robert A. Emmons, University of California and Davis Michael E. McCullough, University of Miami

How Al-Anon Works: for Families and Friends of Alcoholics, Al-Anon Family Groups, chapter 10

Session: THANKFULNESS

Introduction

Read, *"In this session we're going to talk about thankfulness. Can we be grateful in the middle of the nightmare we're going through with our child? Is it possible to give thanks, even though it's the last thing we want to do? Could this be the way to lighten our burden and gain a new perspective?*

Ask *a volunteer to read the scripture and paragraph in their notebook and then discuss it.*

"Give thanks in all circumstances; for this is the will of God in Christ Jesus for you" (1 Thessalonians 5:18).

This Bible passage tells us to be thankful no matter what is happening in our lives. This is what God wants us to do. It's hard when we're going through painful experiences. However, with dependence on God and practice, we can learn to give thanks anyway. By giving thanks we refocus our attention on positive things, lighten our burdens, and increase our awareness of God's activity in our lives.

Definition

Ask *a volunteer to read the definition then* **ask,** *"How does it make you feel to think about being thankful? Explain your answer."*

Thankfulness—to express gratitude for something or to someone, usually by saying, "Thank you"; a feeling of appreciation for kindness or thoughtfulness.

Ask *volunteers to take turns reading the following paragraphs and encourage discussion.*

- Researchers with The Gratitude and Thankfulness Project in 2003 found that people who keep gratitude journals on a weekly basis exercised more frequently, reported fewer physical symptoms, felt better about their lives as a whole, and were more optimistic about the upcoming week compared to those who recorded hassles or neutral life events.

- When things go wrong and life is hard, God wants us to trust Him. When life is out of control, look for something to be thankful for. Gratitude in hard times is a supernatural response. It's unnatural, but it has the power to lift us up above our circumstances. Our knee-jerk response is to grumble and complain. Pretty soon we begin to feel sorry for ourselves and start having a big pity party. Before we know it, we've turned into a critical, cynical, pessimistic person.

- A negative, complaining spirit only hurts us and others in our lives. We aren't very pleasant to be around. People begin to avoid us. What we need to do is reaffirm our trust in God and shift our focus. When we do this, our pessimistic attitude begins to reverse, regardless of how we feel.

- Give thanks to God even though it's the opposite of what you want to do. It sounds crazy, but if you at least try, you'll slowly begin to come out of the fog of negativism. You'll begin moving toward a more peaceful place. It is possible.

- Thankfulness is a key to uplift the troubled heart. "Do not be anxious about anything, but in every situation, by prayer and petition, with thanksgiving, present your requests to God. And the peace of God, which transcends all understanding, will guard your hearts and your minds in Christ Jesus" (Philippians 4:6–7).

How to Develop an Attitude of Thankfulness

Say, "We're going to take the next ten minutes to do an individual activity. I want you to write down everything you can think of that you're thankful for today. It can be as simple as "I got out of bed this morning," "I had wonderful parents," or "I heard a song on the radio that encouraged me." There is a page in the Parent Notebook called "I'm Thankful For", to do this activity. Tell everyone to turn to this page.

If possible, play relaxing music in the background.

After ten minutes, call the group back together and ask, "Would anyone like to share how this activity affected you?" Encourage parents to be honest with their feelings regardless of the impact.

Reflection

Ask, "What helpful insights did you gain from this session?"

At Home Gratitude Challenge

Say, "We want to challenge each of you to start a gratitude journal. Write down at least one thing you're thankful for every day, no matter how insignificant it may seem. When you have a bad day, get out your journal and read over past entries. Over time, notice to how your attitude begins to change."

If you have not already done so, give each parent a small notepad to use for their gratitude journal or give one to those who don't have one yet. If you have time, you could tell parents to write down something in their notepad before you pray.

Prayer

NOTES

Session 20

SELF-CARE

SELF-CARE

Session Aim:

Parents will recognize that they tend to neglect their self-care, which opens the door to developing bigger problems. They will discover how and why they need to take better care of themselves, instead of focusing on the person they have no control over.

Key Principles:

When our children struggle, it takes a toll on us. We need to stop ignoring ourselves and begin to engage in self-care activities. When we do, we'll find moments of refreshment and be able to persevere in a healthier way.

Scripture:

Matthew 11:28
"Come to me, all you who are weary and burdened, and I will give you rest."

Isaiah 40:29
"He gives strength to the weary and increases the power of the weak."

Resources:

You're Not Alone conference, Dr. John Vawter

Al-Anon literature

Materials Needed:

One index card for each parent.

Session: SELF-CARE

Introduction

Ask a volunteer to read, *"When we're consumed with our children and their troubles, we tend to neglect our own well-being. Sometimes we become martyrs as we try to save them. This creates huge amounts of stress that will ultimately take a toll on us. If we don't make the effort to take better care of ourselves, then we may end up sick—emotionally, physically, or spiritually. We need to be intentional about our self-care."*

Ask, *"In what ways have you neglected yourself?"*

Ways We Are Affected

Ask volunteers to read the list.

- We can't sleep or we sleep too much.

- We can't eat or we eat too much.

- We watch a lot of television.

- We become depressed and lethargic. It's difficult to get up in the morning, keep moving, and go to work.

- We withdraw and isolate.

- We don't care about our appearance.

- We experience more physical ailments.

- We're full of anxiety and can't stop worrying. We obsess over our child's behavior.

- We become disillusioned, stop going to church, maybe stop praying—even believing. "Why bother. It hasn't made any difference."

- We doubt God's goodness. "If He's so good, why did He let this happen?"

- Our relationships suffer under the strain: spouse, other children, relatives, and friends.

- We have difficulty concentrating and focusing at work. Our productivity suffers.

Ask, *"Which of these have you experienced?"*

Self-Care Activities

Read, *"What are some ways we can take care of ourselves?" Encourage discussion.*

Ask *volunteers to read the list. Guide discussion.*

- Get plenty of rest—nap if you feel the need.

- Eat healthy. Watch your sugar, fat, and caffeine intake. Drink more water. Eat fresh fruits and vegetables. Don't skip meals. Protein and fiber are good sources of energy.

- Make yourself exercise—at least take a fifteen-minute walk several times a week. Ask a friend to join you or find a group. Exercise releases endorphins in the brain, a natural mood lifter.

- Talk to a counselor, therapist, or clergyperson.

- Find a way to connect with God: reading the Bible, prayer, worship, etc. If this is hard and concentration is lacking, try these approaches: listen to music, appreciate nature, listen to an audio Bible through an app on your electronic device, or read prayers from books written especially for hurting parents.

- Make an appointment with your doctor for a physical if you have persistent physical symptoms.

- Get involved in a support group.

- Simplify your life. Cut back on as many nonessential activities as possible. You need all your reserves to cope with the circumstances.

- Reach out to a few trusted, nonjudgmental friends. Share honestly with them. No more hiding or stuffing your feelings. Secrets make us sick. Limit the amount of time you allow yourself to talk about your child. Too much is counterproductive.

- Enjoy a hobby or cultivate a new one. It's a positive distraction.

- Make time for fun. Do what refreshes you.

Ask, *"Which of these have you tried and how did it help?*

Reflection

Ask *the group to read this Bible verse in unison:*

"He gives strength to the weary and increases the power of the weak" (Isaiah 40:29).

Give each parent an index card. **Ask,** *"What do you want to start doing or do more of to take better care of yourself? Take a few minutes right now to make a list on your index card. Take it with you as a reminder. If you can't think of anything, ask God to show you."*

Prayer

NOTES

Session 21

HOPE

HOPE

Session Aim:

Parents will grow in their understanding of hope and begin to develop a hope they can count on.

Key Principles:

Firm hope is built on who God is, what He has done, and what He has promised. Fragile hope is less certain, since it involves the free will of another person.

Scripture:

Romans 15:13

"May the God of hope fill you will all joy and peace as you trust in him, so that you may overflow with hope by the power of the Holy Spirit."

Psalm 62:5

"Yes, my soul, find rest in God; my hope comes from him."

Proverbs 3:5–6

"Trust in the Lord with all your heart and lean not on your own understanding; in all your ways submit to him, and he will make your paths straight."

John 14:1 ESV

"Do not let your hearts be troubled. Believe in God; believe also in me."

Daniel 3:17–18

"If we are thrown into the blazing furnace, the God we serve is able to deliver us from it, and he will deliver us from Your Majesty's hand. But even if he does not, we want you to know, Your Majesty, that we will not serve your gods or worship the image of gold you have set up."

Romans 8:24–25

"For in this hope we were saved. But hope that is seen is no hope at all. Who hopes for what they already have? But if we hope for what we do not yet have, we wait for it patiently."

Psalm 147:11

"The LORD delights in those who fear him, who put their hope in his unfailing love."

Resources:

The Hope of a Homecoming by O'Rourke and Sauer, chapter 13

A New Kind of Normal by Carol, chapter 4

Will Your Prodigal Come Home? by Jeff Lucas, chapter 5

Hope and Help for the Addicted by Jeff VanVonderen, chapter 10

Holding on to Hope and The One Year Book of Hope by Nancy Guthrie

Materials Needed:

A sheet of paper or index card for each parent.

Promises to Claim—to be used in the Hope Activity. This is found in your appendix and in the appendix of the parent notebook.

Session: HOPE

Introduction

Hand out *an index card or sheet of paper to each person.* **Ask,** *"When you think about your child, what hopes do you have? Take the next few minutes to write them down." After a few minutes encourage parents to share their list.*

Ask, *"What is hope? How do you define it?" Encourage discussion.*

Ask *a volunteer to read these definitions. "A feeling of expectation and desire for a certain thing to happen; a feeling of trust (www.dictionary.com)"; wanting something to come true in the future; to anticipate, look for or desire something or someone.*

Ask, *"Which parts of the definition stand out to you?"*

Firm and Fragile Hope

Ask volunteers to read each statement below, pausing after each one for the group to decide if it is a firm or fragile hope. Allow discussion.

- God loves and cares more about our child than we do and will never stop seeking them.

- God is my ally not my adversary.

- I trained my child in the faith and they will return to it someday.

- One day my child will be free from their addiction, mental health issues, self-injury, etc.

- I am not alone. God promised never to leave me or forsake me.

- If I believe and pray earnestly, then my child won't experience negative or lifelong consequences.

After the group discussion, ask volunteers to read the following statements and allow for comments.

Firm hope needs to be in who God is and what He has done for us in Christ. He will be with us; He will help us, and will use all our pain to make us more like His Son. This is His ultimate goal.

Firm hope is also in the promises of God, in what He says He will do for us in His Word.

Hope is real. God can do the impossible. He transforms lives every day. But there is a tension here—another person's free will is involved. We have no control over what they choose. Our challenge is not to hold too tightly to the hopes we have for our child because this is a fragile hope. Keep trusting for the impossible, but open your hand to receive from God whatever He allows.

We want to be able to say, like the three men of God who were about to be thrown into a fiery furnace: "If we are thrown into the blazing furnace, the God we serve is able to deliver us from it, and he will deliver us from Your Majesty's hand. But even if he does not, we want you to know, Your Majesty, that we will not serve your gods or worship the image of gold you have set up."

Our goal is to affirm, "even if he does not . . ." "If my child never changes in my lifetime, or at all, I will still trust You, Lord.

154

Hope Quotes

Ask volunteers to read the following quotes then **ask,** *"Which ones impressed you?"*

"We're not necessarily doubting that God will do what's best for us; we are wondering how painful the best will turn out to be." — C.S. Lewis

"Our hope should not be in anyone's behavior or the timing of our struggles." — Mark Gregston

"Our hope is in God alone. We trust him with the what, the how, and the when of the working out of His plan." — Dena Yohe

"Hope is the certainty that God cares for our children more than we do and will never stop seeking them." — Dena Yohe

"We must accept finite disappointment, but never lose infinite hope." — Martin Luther King Jr.

"There is no medicine like hope, no incentive so great, no tonic so powerful as expectations of something better tomorrow." — Dietrich Bonhoeffer

Hope Activity

Say, "An acrostic for *hope* is—**H**olding **O**n to **P**romises **E**xpectantly.

Read, "There are over seven thousand promises in the Bible. Learning many of them will help us build a firm hope we can count on. As a group, let's brainstorm some of these promises. The Bible references or exact wording isn't necessary. Simply share what comes to your mind."

After allowing time for brainstorming, refer to the Promises found in the appendix, or you could share the verses in your preparation section.

Prayer

NOTES

Session 22

RESILIENCE

RESILIENCE

Session Aim:

To understand what resilience is and how it can be developed.

Key Principles:

Difficulties in life stretch us, sometimes to our breaking point. Becoming resilient helps us recover and bounce back, rather than turning into a rigid, hardened, and defeated person.

Scripture:

Romans 15:4

"For everything that was written in the past was written to teach us, so that through the endurance taught in the Scriptures and the encouragement they provide we might have hope."

James 5:11 NASB

"We count those blessed who endured."

Hebrews 12:3

"Consider him who endured such opposition from sinners, so that you will not grow weary and lose heart."

2 Corinthians 4:16

"Therefore we do not lose heart. Though outwardly we are wasting away, yet inwardly we are being renewed day by day."

2 Corinthians 4:8–9 ESV

"We are afflicted in every way, but not crushed; perplexed, but not driven to despair; persecuted, but not forsaken; struck down, but not destroyed."

Galatians 6:9 NASB

"Let us not lose heart in doing good, for in due time we will reap if we do not grow weary."

Resources:

Do Not Lose Heart by Dave and Jan Dravecky

When I Lay My Isaac Down by Carol Kent, chapter 5

A Resilient Life by Gordon MacDonald

Materials Needed: (optional)

A rubber band for each participant

A balloon and balloon pump (unless you choose to play a movie clip)

Fiddler on the Roof video clip or other relevant movie scene about reaching your breaking point or being stretched too far

Session: RESILIENCE

Introduction

Say, *"Today we're going to talk about resilience. What do you think it is to be resilient? Encourage discussion.*

Tell *the group to open their Parent Notebook to this session and ask a volunteer to read the definition.*

Definition

The capacity to recover quickly from difficulties; elasticity; able to bounce back, adapt, and change when stretched.

Ask, *"What are some things or objects that are resilient?"*

Possible answers: rubber band, trampoline, elastic waistband, headband, ponytail holder, wristband, an exercise or tension ball, bungee cord/strap, human skin (pregnancy), balloon, silly putty.

Give *everyone a rubber band to hold during the session and tell them this is to help them think about becoming resilient.*

Discussion Questions

Ask the following questions allowing time for discussion after each.

In what ways have you felt stretched or bent out of shape?

Is this a quality you think we need? Why or why not?

If we're stretched too far we'll break. Do you have a breaking point? What is it?

Optional illustration for being stretched too far.

*Use either a balloon or video clip to illustrate stretching something too far to the breaking point. Put the balloon on the pump and blow it up until it pops. Or, use the **Fiddler on the Roof** video segment where the father, Tevye, tells his daughter, "If I bend too far, I'll break!"*

How Can We Become Resilient?

Say, "We don't want you to stretch too far so that you break. How can we become more resilient?"

Ask volunteers to take turns reading the list.

1. Maintain emotional health—not allow emotional, physical, or verbal abuse.

2. Maintain physical health—good diet, adequate rest, manage medical needs, exercise regularly; releases endorphins and naturally improves a sense of well-being.

3. Know and be confident about our true identity—who we are (a child of God) and who we belong to (God).

4. Distinguish between truth and lies; focus on the positive; avoid negative, critical thinking.

5. Know our eternal destiny—heaven; with God forever.

6. Be part of a community—a reliable support system; strong friendships with trustworthy, caring, nonjudgmental people; church, Bible studies, or support groups.

7. Know our limits and enforce wise boundaries; no enabling or overhelping; know when to say no and not give in.

8. Refuse to isolate in times of crisis and distress; willing to let others know when we're in need; share our struggles with openness and authenticity.

9. Cultivate or pursue a hobby: music, art, reading, gardening, sports (fishing, boating, golf, bowling, swimming, walking, hiking, biking, billiards, tennis, etc.), crafts or sewing, pets, photography, woodworking, etc.

10. Know yourself well; able to identify feelings and take opportunities to talk about them honestly with a friend, clergy, life coach, counselor, or in a small group/support group setting.

11. Cultivate a strong faith in God and grow in the relationship.

12. Develop a thankful disposition—an attitude of gratitude. Make a list and add to it daily. Helps develop contentment and even joy in the midst of trials.

13. Make time for fun—laughter is good medicine.

14. Do whatever refreshes you for the pure enjoyment of it.

Ask the following questions and encourage sharing.

"Which ones have you found helpful?"

"What would you add to this list?"

"What would you like to start doing?"

Scripture

Say, "Let's read these verses out loud together."

Romans 15:4
"For everything that was written in the past was written to teach us, so that through the endurance taught in the Scriptures and the encouragement they provide we might have hope."

James 5:11 NASB
"We count those blessed who endured."

Hebrews 12:3

"Consider him who endured such opposition from sinners, so that you will not grow weary and lose heart."

2 Corinthians 4:16

"Therefore we do not lose heart. Though outwardly we are wasting away, yet inwardly we are being renewed day by day."

2 Corinthians 4:8–9 ESV

"We are afflicted in every way, but not crushed; perplexed, but not driven to despair; persecuted, but not forsaken; struck down, but not destroyed."

Galatians 6:9 NASB

"Let us not lose heart in doing good, for in due time we will reap if we do not grow weary."

Reflection

Read, *"The opposite of resilience is rigid, hardened, or defeated. Has your journey had this effect on you? We may need resilience more than we thought. Take a few quiet minutes to talk to God. Ask Him to help you become more resilient."*

*If there's time, **ask**, "What is your take-away from this session?"*

Prayer

NOTES

Appendix

THE SERENITY PRAYER

GOD, grant me the serenity

To accept the things I cannot change;

Courage to change the things I can;

And wisdom to know the difference.

Living one day at a time;

Enjoying one moment at a time;

Accepting hardships as the pathway to peace;

Taking, as He did, this sinful world as it is

Not as I would have it;

Trusting that he will make all things right

If I surrender to his will;

That I will be reasonably happy in this life;

And supremely happy with him

Forever in the next.

Amen.

-Reinhold Niebhur

THE LORD'S PRAYER

Our Father who is in heaven, hallowed be Your name.

Your kingdom come, Your will be done, on earth as it is in heaven.

Give us this day our daily bread. And forgive us our debts, as we also have forgiven our debtors.

And do not lead us into temptation, but deliver us from evil.

For Yours is the kingdom and the power and the glory forever. Amen.

I BLESS YOU PRAYER

I bless you with unwavering hope.

Romans 15:13

"May the God of hope fill you with all joy and peace
As you trust in Him,
So that you may overflow with hope,
By the power of the Holy Spirit."

I bless you with unshakable faith, so that no matter what happens, you're convinced God will be with you.

I bless you with unspeakable joy that defies reason.

I bless you with unfaltering peace in every circumstance, because you know the Living God is your constant companion.

I bless you with the unthinkable, supernatural ability to trust, no matter what you see happening.

I bless you with unimaginable, divine strength that far surpasses your own, sufficient to carry you through anything and everything that should ever come your way.

I bless you with an unusual outpouring of the Holy Spirit, so that by His unlimited power, the "God of hope" will give you abundant joy, peace, hope, and strength as you walk this difficult path with your child.

I bless you in the beautiful name of Jesus.

Amen.

Dena Yohe 2013

DECLARATION OF RELEASE

We are selfish by nature. Nobody had to teach us to want things our way. When someone doesn't do things our way, we try to change them, to make them conform to what we believe is right and best. We may feel that someone is heading in the wrong direction, and we want to get him on the track we believe to be right. We may call it concern, but it really may be selfishness and control. No matter how right we may be, we are wrong to try to control others and make them conform to our desires, even our godly desires. It is God's job to change people, not ours. Be careful of trying to control others. Give them to God so He can accomplish His perfect will in their lives.

Make this declaration of release[2] as often as necessary:

Because Jesus Christ is my Lord, I free you from my anxiety, fears, and control. I trust the Holy Spirit to lead you and show you the way that is right for you—the way of love, joy, and peace and all that salvation includes.

I place you at God's throne of grace. I cannot force my will on you. I cannot live your life for you. I give you to God the Father, Son, and Holy Spirit. You are a very special person. As much as I love you, God loves you more. Your life today is totally in His hands, and I trust Him with it.

In Jesus' name…

I release you from my expectations,

I place you on open palms to the Lord,

I give you my blessings,

I let you go.

In His love,

Signed_____

Date _____

"It is God who works in you to will and to act according to his good purpose; being confident of this, that he who began a good work in you will carry it on to completion until the day of Christ Jesus" (Philippians 2:13, 1:6).

[2] Used with permission from @Sylvia Gunter, The Father's Business, P. O. Box 380333, Birmingham, AL 35238 www.thefathersbusiness.com. Email: info@thefathersbusiness.com

EIGHT TRUTHS FOR YOUR HEART

Is fear ruling your life too much? When you really think about it are you afraid to say "no", afraid to not help, afraid to show your anger or hurt, afraid to show you're confusion, afraid of the unknowns, of what's next, of not being in control, of having no guarantees?

<u>Remember these 8 truths for your heart:</u>

1. God is in control, even when it doesn't look like it.

2. You are not alone.

3. You and your child are in His hands.

4. No matter what happens you will be okay.

5. With God's help you can handle anything.

6. You can reach out to others for help.

7. You can reach out to God in prayer anytime, anywhere.

8. You can let go and let God work.

Al-Anon says, "We turn our will and our life over to the care of God . . ." That is exactly what we must keep doing—over and over again.

Psalm 71:2
"Be my rock of refuge to which I can always go..."

THE REST OF VICTORY

THERE IS NOTHING – NO CIRCUMSTANCE, NO TESTING –

THAT CAN EVER TOUCH ME, UNTIL FIRST OF ALL,

IT HAS GONE PAST GOD AND PAST CHRIST, RIGHT THROUGH TO ME.

IF IT HAS COME THAT FAR, IT HAS COME WITH A GREAT PURPOSE WHICH I MAY

NOT UNDERSTAND AT THE MOMENT.

BUT AS I REFUSE TO BECOME PANICKY,

AS I LIFT UP MY EYES TO HIM AND ACCEPT IT

AS COMING FROM THE THRONE OF GOD

FOR SOME GREAT PURPOSE OR BLESSING TO MY OWN HEART,

NO SORROW WILL EVER DISTURB ME,

NO TRIAL WILL EVER DISARM ME,

NO CIRCUMSTANCE WILL CAUSE ME TO FRET.

FOR I SHALL REST IN THE JOY OF WHAT MY LORD IS.

AND THAT IS THE REST OF VICTORY!

ALAN REDPATH

PROMISES

❖ *I am not alone. God is with me and will never leave me or forsake me.*

"God has said, 'Never will I leave you; never will I forsake you' " (Hebrews 13:5b).

"The LORD Almighty is with us; the God of Jacob is our fortress" (Psalm 46: 7).

"So do not fear, for I am with you; do not be dismayed, for I am your God. I will strengthen you and help you; I will uphold you with my righteous right hand" (Isaiah 41:10a).

"And teaching them to obey everything I have commanded you. And surely I am with you always, to the very end of the age" (Matthew 28:20).

❖ *God loves me and my child with an unfailing, eternal love.*

"For God so loved the world that he gave his one and only Son, that whoever believes in him shall not perish but have eternal life" (John 3:16).

❖ *I have all the help I need from the Holy Spirit – a Helper, Advocate, Counselor, and Comforter.*

"And I will ask the Father, and he will give you another Counselor to be with you forever" (John 14:16).

"But the Counselor, the Holy Spirit, whom the Father will send in my name, will teach you all things and will remind you of everything I have said to you" (John 14:26).

"When the Counselor comes, whom I will send to you from the Father, the Spirit of truth who goes out from the Father, he will testify about me" (John 15:26).

"But I tell you the truth: It is for your good that I am going away. Unless I go away, the Counselor will not come to you; but if I go, I will send him to you" (John 16:7).

❖*Jesus prays for me all the time.*

"Therefore he is able to save completely those who come to God through him, because he always lives to intercede for them" (Hebrews 7:25).

❖ *God wants to help my child, will never stop seeking him/her. He does not want them to perish.*

"The Lord is not slow in keeping his promise, as some understand slowness. He is patient with you, not wanting anyone to perish, but everyone to come to repentance" (2 Peter 3:9).

❖*God is patient and slow to anger with my child.*

"And he passed in front of Moses, proclaiming, 'The LORD, the LORD, the compassionate and gracious God, slow to anger, abounding in love and faithfulness" ' (Exodus 34:6).

"Love is patient, love is kind. It does not envy, it does not boast, it is not proud" (1 Corinthians 13:4).

❖*God always hears my prayers.*

"The LORD is far from the wicked but he hears the prayer of the righteous" (Proverbs 15:29).

❖ *God will accomplish His purposes in my life.*

"The LORD Almighty has sworn, 'Surely, as I have planned, so it will be, and as I have purp d, so it will stand' " (Isaiah 14: 24).

❖ *God will give me the strength and endurance I need.*

"He gives strength to the weary and increases the power of the weak. Even youths grow tired and weary, and young men stumble and fall" (Isaiah 40:29-30).

❖ *I can be joyful in trails.*

"Though the fig tree does not bud and there are no grapes on the vines, though the olive crop fails and the fields produce no food, though there are no sheep in the pen and no cattle in the stalls, yet I will rejoice in the LORD, I will be joyful in God my Savior. The Sovereign LORD is my strength; he makes my feet like the feet of a deer, he enables me to go on the heights" (Habakkuk 3:17-19).

❖ *I don't need to worry about anything, pray instead to have peace of heart and mind.*

"Do not be anxious about anything, but in everything, by prayer and petition, with thanksgiving, present your requests to God. And the peace of God, which transcends all understanding, will guard your hearts and your minds in Christ Jesus" (Philippians 4:6-7).

❖ *There is purpose for our pain.*

"I wrote as I did so that when I came I should not be distressed by those who ought to make me rejoice. I had confidence in all of you, that you would all share my joy. For I wrote you out of great distress and anguish of heart and with many tears, not to grieve you but to let you know the depth of my love for you" (2 Corinthians 2:3-5).

"But we have this treasure in jars of clay to show that this all-surpassing power is from God and not from us. We are hard pressed on every side, but not crushed; perplexed, but not in despair; persecuted, but not abandoned; struck down, but not destroyed. We always carry around in our body the death of Jesus, so that the life of Jesus may also be revealed in our body" (2 Corinthians 4:7-10).

❖ *There is always hope.*

"This is what the LORD says: 'Restrain your voice from weeping and your eyes from tears, for your work will be rewarded,' declares the LORD. 'They will return from the land of the enemy. So there is hope for your future,' declares the LORD. 'Your children will return to their own land' " (Jeremiah 31:16-17).

"Why are you downcast, O my soul? Why so disturbed within me? Put your hope in God, for I will yet praise him, my Savior and my God" (Psalm 42:5).

"But as for me, I will always have hope; I will praise you more and more. My mouth will tell of your righteousness, of your salvation all day long, though I know not its measure" (Psalm 71:14-15).

❖ *God will lead and guide me.*

"The LORD is my shepherd; I shall not be in want. He makes me lie down in green pastures, he leads me beside quiet waters, he restores my soul. He guides me in paths of righteousness for his name's sake" (Psalm 23:1-3).

"They will neither hunger nor thirst, nor will the desert heat or the sun beat upon them. He who has compassion on them will guide them and lead them beside springs of water" (Isaiah 49:10).

❖ *God will give me wisdom.*

"If any of you lacks wisdom, he should ask God, who gives generously to all without finding fault, and it will be given to him" (James 1:5).

❖ *This pain won't last forever.*

"For I consider that the sufferings of this present time are not worthy to be compared with the glory that is to be revealed to us" (Romans 8:18).

"And I heard a loud voice from the throne saying, "Now the dwelling of God is with men, and he will live with them. They will be his people, and God himself will be with them and be their God. He will wipe every tear from their eyes. There will be no more death or mourning or crying or pain, for the old order of things has passed away" (Revelation 21:3-4).

❖ *God is still good no matter what.*

"How great is your goodness, which you have stored up for those who fear you, which you bestow in the sight of men on those who take refuge in you" (Psalm 31:19).

"When you give it to them, they gather it up; when you open your hand, they are satisfied with good things" (Psalm 104:28).

"Be at rest once more, O my soul, for the LORD has been good to you" (Psalm 116:7).

❖ *Nothing will ever separate me from the love of God.*

"For I am convinced that neither death nor life, neither angels nor demons, neither the present nor the future, nor any powers, neither height nor depth, nor anything else in all creation, will be able to separate us from the love of God that is in Christ Jesus our Lord" (Romans 8:38-39).

❖ *God cares about my pain. He weeps with me, collects my tears in His bottle; wipes my tears.*

"Cast all your anxiety on him because he cares for you" (1 Peter 5:7).

"Record my lament; list my tears on your scroll - are they not in your record?" (Psalm 56:8).

"And I heard a loud voice from the throne saying, 'Now the dwelling of God is with men, and he will live with them. They will be his people, and God himself will be with them and be their God. He will wipe every tear from their eyes. There will be no more death or mourning or crying or pain, for the old order of things has passed away' " (Revelation 21:3-4).

❖ *I will survive this because the Lord is my help and strength.*

"God is our refuge and strength, an ever-present help in trouble. Therefore we will not fear, though the earth give way and the mountains fall into the heart of the sea . . ." (Psalm 46:1-2).

"So do not fear, for I am with you; do not be dismayed, for I am your God. I will strengthen you and help you; I will uphold you with my righteous right hand" (Isaiah 41:10).

❖ *God is trustworthy and faithful.*

"For great is his love toward us, and the faithfulness of the LORD endures forever. Praise the LORD" (Psalm 117:2).

❖ *God can do the impossible.*

"The disciples were even more amazed, and said to each other, 'Who then can be saved?' Jesus looked at them and said, 'With man this is impossible, but not with God; all things are possible with God' " (Mark 10:26-27).

❖ *God is able to do more than I think or imagine.*

"Now to him who is able to do immeasurably more than all we ask or imagine, according to his power that is at work within us" (Ephesians 3:20).

❖ *God gives sufficient grace each day and His power for our weakness.*

"But he said to me, 'My grace is sufficient for you, for my power is made perfect in weakness.' Therefore I will boast all the more gladly about my weaknesses, so that Christ's power may rest on me. That is why, for Christ's sake, I delight in weaknesses, in insults, in hardships, in persecutions, in difficulties. For when I am weak, then I am strong" (2 Corinthians 12: 9-10).

❖ *God will sustain me through this hard time.*

"Surely God is my help; the Lord is the one who sustains me" (Psalm 54:4).

"Cast your cares on the LORD and he will sustain you; he will never let the righteous fall" (Psalm 55:22).

❖ *God is forgiving and good, abounding in love to all who call on Him.*

"You are forgiving and good, O Lord, abounding in love to all who call to you" (Psalm 86:5).

❖ *Godly sorrow brings repentance that leads to salvation with no regrets.*

"Godly sorrow brings repentance that leads to salvation and leaves no regret, but worldly sorrow brings death" (2 Corinthians 7:10).

❖ *God blesses His people with peace.*

"The LORD gives strength to his people; the LORD blesses his people with peace" (Psalm 29:11).

❖ *When we pray, God will answer.*

"When I called, you answered me; you made me bold and stouthearted" (Psalm 138:3).

❖ *God is close to the brokenhearted and saves those who are crushed in spirit.*

"The LORD is close to the brokenhearted and saves those who are crushed in spirit" (Psalm 34:18).

❖ *God will comfort us in all our troubles.*

"Praise be to the God and Father of our Lord Jesus Christ, the Father of compassion and the God of all comfort, who comforts us in all our troubles, so that we can comfort those in any trouble with the comfort we ourselves have received from God. For just as the sufferings of Christ flow over into our lives, so also through Christ our comfort overflows" (2 Corinthians 1:3-5).

❖ *I can do all that I need to do through the strength of Christ.*

"I can do everything through him who gives me strength" (Philippians 4:13).

❖ *God will restore us again.*

"Though you have made me see troubles, many and bitter, you will restore my life again; from the depths of the earth you will again bring me up. You will increase my honor and comfort me once again" (Psalm 71:20-21).

RECOMMENDED BOOKS AND RESOURCES

General Comfort

Barnes, Emily. *My Cup Overflows…with the Comfort of God's Love*. Eugene, OR: Harvest House, 1998.

Coleman, Bill. *Parents with Broken Hearts: Helping Parents of Prodigals to Cope*. Rev. ed. Winona Lake, IN: BMH Books, revised edition, 2007.

Crabb, Larry. *Shattered Dreams: God's Unexpected Pathway to Joy*. Colorado Springs: WaterBrook, 2001.

Dobson, Dr. James. *When God Doesn't Make Sense*. Carol Stream, IL: Tyndale House, 1993.

Dravecky, Dave. *Do Not Lose Heart: Meditations of Encouragement and Comfort*. Grand Rapids: Zondervan, 2001.

Guthrie, Nancy. *Holding on to Hope: A Pathway Through Suffering to the Heart of God*. Wheaton, IL: Tyndale, 2002.

_____. *The One Year Book of Hope*. Wheaton, IL: Tyndale House, 2005.

Kent, Carol. *A New Kind of Normal: Hope-filled Choices When Life Turns Upside Down*. Nashville: Thomas Nelson, 2007.

Kent, Carol. *When I Lay My Isaac Down: Unshakable Faith in Unthinkable Circumstances*. Colorado Springs: NavPress, 2004.

Lucado, Max. *God Will Use This for Good: Surviving the Mess of Life*. Nashville: Thomas Nelson, 2013.

_____. *It's Not About Me: Rescue from the Life We Thought Would Make Us Happy*. Nashville: Integrity, 2004.

Lucas, Jeff. *Will Your Prodigal Come Home? An Honest Discussion of Struggle and Hope*. Grand Rapids: Zondervan, 2007.

O'Rourke, Brendan, and DeEtte Sauer. *The Hope of a Homecoming: Entrusting Your Prodigal to a Sovereign God*. Colorado Springs: Navpress, 2003.

Thompson, Marjorie J., and Stephen D. Bryant. *Companions in Christ: The Way of Forgiveness: Participants Book*. Nashville: Upper Room, 2002.

Tworkowski, Jamie. *If You Feel Too Much: Thoughts on Things Found and Lost and Hoped For*. New York: Jeremy P. Tarcher, 2015.

Voskamp, Ann. *One Thousand Gifts: A Dare to Live Fully Right Where You Are*. Grand Rapids: Zondervan, 2010.

Vujicic, Nick. *Life Without Limits: Inspiration for a Ridiculously Good Life.* Colorado Springs: WaterBrook, 2010.

Walsh, Sheila. *Life is Tough but God is Faithful.* Nashville: Thomas Nelson, 1999.

Warren, Rick. *The Purpose Driven Life: What on Earth Am I Here For?* Grand Rapids: Zondervan, 2002.

Wright, H. Norman. *Experiencing Grief.* Nashville: B&H Publishing Group, 2004.

_____. *Loving a Prodigal: A Survival Guide for Parents of Rebellious Children.* Colorado Springs: Chariot Victor, 1999.

Yohe, Dena. *You Are Not Alone: Hope for Hurting Parents of Troubled Kids.* Colorado Springs: WaterBrook, 2016.

Yohe, Renee. *Purpose for the Pain.* Orlando, FL: Bonded Books, 2008.

Websites

Hope for Hurting Parents, www.HopeForHurtingParents.com

Prayer

Banks, James. *Prayers for Prodigals: 90 Days of Prayer for Your Child.* Grand Rapids: RBC Ministries, 2011.

Berndt, Jodie. *Praying the Scriptures for Your Teenagers: Discover How to Pray God's Will for Their Lives.* Grand Rapids: Zondervan, 2007.

Cosby, Sharron. *Praying for Your Addicted Loved One: 90 in 90.* Auburn, WA: Bookjolt, 2013.

Logan, Jim. *Reclaiming Surrendered Ground: Protecting Your Family from Spiritual Attacks.* Chicago: Moody: 1995.

Morgan, Robert J. *Moments for Families with Prodigals.* Colorado Springs: NavPress, 2003.

Omartian, Stormie. *The Power of a Praying Parent.* Eugene, OR: Harvest House, 2014.

_____. *The Power of Praying for Your Adult Children.* Eugene, OR: Harvest House, 2009.

Roberts, Lee. *Praying God's Will for My Daughter.* Rev. ed. Nashville: Thomas Nelson, 2002.

_____. *Praying God's Will for My Son.* Rev. ed. Nashville: Thomas Nelson, revised 2002.

Thompson, Janet. *Praying for Your Prodigal Daughter: Hope, Help and Encouragement for Hurting Parents.* New York: Howard Books, 2007.

Websites

Breakthrough, www.intercessors.org

Prayer for Prodigals, http://prayerforprodigals.com, developed by Cru (formerly Campus Crusade for Christ). Request an invitation via e-mail: prayerforprodigals@gmail.com. This is a password-protected site on which you can post prayer requests and receive prayers back from participants by e-mail. It's full of resources: Scripture verses, prayers, recommended books, inspirational devotionals, and places for help around the country for many issues (therapeutic boarding schools for teens, drug and alcohol rehabs, wilderness camps for youth, eating disorder programs, and more).

Facebook pages: 365 Days of Prayers for Prodigals; Prayer for Prodigals; and The Prodigal Hope Network.

Addiction

Alcoholics Anonymous. *The Big Book.* 4th ed. New York: Alcoholics Anonymous World Services, 2001. Available at meetings and online. Brochures available at meetings.

Al-Anon literature. *Courage to Change and One Day at a Time in Al-Anon II.* Available at meetings and online. Brochures available at meetings.

Conyers, Beverly. *Addict in the Family: Stories of Loss, Hope, and Recovery.* Center City, MN: Hazelden, 2003.

_____. *Everything Changes: Help for Families of Newly Recovering Addicts.* Center City, MN: Hazelden, 2009.

Hayden, Karilee and Wendi Hayden English. *Wild Child, Waiting Mom: Finding Hope in the Midst of Heartache.* Wheaton, IL: Tyndale, 2006.

Hersh, Sharon. *The Last Addiction: Why Self-Help if Not Enough, Own Your Desire, Live Beyond Recovery, Find Lasting Freedom.* Colorado Springs; WaterBrook, 2008.

White, John. *Parents in Pain: Overcoming the Hurt and Frustration of Problem Children.* Downers Grove, IL: Intervarsity Press, 1979.

VanVonderen, Jeff. *Hope and Help for the Addicted.* Grand Rapids: Revell, 2004.

Vawter, John, ed. *Hit by a Ton of Bricks.* Little Rock, AR: Family Life Publishing, 2003.

White, John. *Parents in Pain: A Book of Comfort and Counsel.* Downers Grove, IL: InterVarsity, 1979.

Websites

About Alcoholism, www.aboutalcoholism.org.

Al-Anon Family Groups, www.al-anon.org.

Celebrate Recovery, www.celebraterecovery.com.

Co-Dependents Anonymous; www.coda.org.

Nar-Anon Family Groups, www.nar-anon.org.

Boundaries

Adams, Jane. *When Our Grown Kids Disappoint Us: Letting Go of Their Problems, Loving Them Anyway, and Getting On with Our Lives.* New York: Free Press, 2003.

Beattie, Melodie. *CoDependent No More: How to Stop Controlling Others and Start Caring for Yourself.* Center City, MN: Hazelden, 1992.

Bottke, Allison. *Setting Boundaries with Your Adult Children.* Eugene, OR: Harvest House, 2008.

Cloud, Henry, and John Townsend. *Boundaries: When to Say Yes, When to Say No to Take Control of Your Life.* Grand Rapids: Zondervan, 1992.

Friends in Recovery. *The Twelve Steps for Christian from Addictive and Other Dysfunctional Families: Based on Biblical Teachings.* San Diego: Recovery Publications, 1988.

Rubin, Charles. *Don't Let Your Kids Kill You: A Survival Guide for Parents of Drug Addicts and Alcoholics.* 3rd ed. Petaluma, CA: NewCentury, 2010.

For Parents of Troubled Adolescents

Dobson, James. *The New Strong-Willed Child: Birth Through Adolescence.* Wheaton, IL: Tyndale, 2004.

Gregston, Mark. *When Your Teen is Struggling.* Eugene, OR: Harvest House, 2007. See also the website www.heartlightministries.org.

Hersh, Sharon. *Mom, Everyone Else Does! Becoming Your Daughter's Ally in Responding to Peer Pressure to Drink, Smoke, and Use Drugs.* Colorado Springs: WaterBrook, 2005.

_____. *Mom I Feel Fat! Becoming Your Daughter's Ally in Developing a Healthy Body Image.* Colorado Springs: Shaw, 2001.

_____. *Mom Everyone Else Does! Becoming Your Daughter's Ally Through the Emotional Ups and /downs of Adolescence.* Colorado Springs: WaterBrook, 2004.

_____. *Mom, Sex is No Big Deal! Becoming Your Daughter's Ally in Developing a Healthy Sexual Identity.* Colorado Springs: Shaw, 2006.

Jantz, Gregory L. *When Your Teenager Becomes The Stranger in Your House.* Colorado Springs: David C. Cook, 2011.

Scott, Buddy. *Relief for Hurting Parents: What to Do and How to Think When You're Having Trouble with Your Kids.* Nashville: Oliver-Nelson Books, 1989. See also author's website: www.buddyscott.com.

Tripp, David. *Age of Opportunity: A Biblical Guide to Parenting Teens*. Phillipsburg, NJ: P&R Publishing, 1997, 2001. See also author's website: www.paultripp.com.

Website

Dr. Dobson's Family Talk, http://drjamesdobson.org.

Bullying

Bullying in a Cyber World, Grades 4 to 5. Rowley, MA: Didax, 2012. Additional materials are available for parents and schools.

Bullying in a Cyber World, Grades 6 to 8. (Rowley, MA: Didax, 2012). Additional materials are available for parents and schools.

Gerali, Dr. Steve. *What Do I Do When: Teenagers Encounter Bullying and Violence?* Grand Rapids: Zondervan, 2009.

Mayo Clinic Staff. *"Bullying: Help Your Child Handle a Bully."* August 23, 2013. www.mayoclinic.org/healthy-living/childrens-health/in-depth/bullying/art-20044918?pg=1.

Miller, Cindy, and Cynthia Lowen. *The Essential Guide to Bullying: Prevention and Intervention: Protecting Children and Teens from Physical, Emotional, and Online Bullying*. New York: Alpha Books, 2012.

National Education Association. *Bully Free: It Starts with Me*. The National Education Association (NEA; www.nea.org) program to stop bullying in public schools.

Students Against Being Bullied, SABB Inc., www.studentsagainstbeingbullied.org, offers antibullying programs that can be used in schools.

van der Zande, Irene. *"Face Bullying with Confidence: 8 KidPower Skills We Can Use Right Away."* Santa Cruz, CA: KidPower, 2011.

_____. *Kidpower Solutions*. Santa Cruz, CA: Kidpower, 2010.

Mental Health

Alcorn, Nancy. *Starved: Mercy for Eating Disorders*. Enumclaw, WA: Winepress Publishing, 2007.

Amador, Xavier. *I Am Not Sick, I Don't Need Help: How to Help Someone with Mental Illness Accept Treatment.* Peconic, NY: VidaPress, 2010. See also the website www.leapinstitute.org.

Bengtson, Michelle. *Hope Prevails: Insights from a Doctor's Personal Journey through Depression.* Grand Rapids: Revell, 2016.

Comer, John Mark. *My Name is Hope: Anxiety, Depression, and Life after Melancholy.* Portland, OR: Graphe, 2011.

Duke, Patty and Gloria Hochman. *A Brilliant Madness: Living with Manic-Depressive Illness.* New York, NY: Bantam, 1992.

Evans, Dwight L., and Linda Wasmer Andrews. *If Your Adolescent Has Depression or Bipolar Disorder: An Essential Resource for Parents.* New York: Oxford University Press, 2006.

Federman, Russ and J. Anderson Thompson, *Facing Bipolar: The Young Adult's Guide to Dealing with Bipolar Disorder.* Oakland, CA: New Harbinger, 2010.

Foa, Edna, and Linda Wasmer Linda Abdrews. *If Your Adolescent Has Depression or Bipolar Disorder: An Essential Resource for Parents.* New York: Oxford University Press, 2006.

Haughton, Debbie. "What Is EMDR and Can It Help My Child?" *Hope for Hurting Parents* (blog). http://HopeforHurtingParents.com/2014/06/18/what-is-emdr-and-can-it-help-my-child.

Hornbacher, Marya. *Wasted: A Memoir of Anorexia and Bulimia.* New York,: HarperCollins, 1999.

Jamison, Kay Redfield. *An Unquiet Mi*nd. New York: Knopf, 1995.

Levine, Jerome, and Irene S. Levine. *Schizophrenia for Dummies.* Hoboken, NJ: Wiley, 2009.

Mason, Paul T. MS and Randi Kreger. *Stop Walking on Eggshells: Taking Your Life Back When Someone You Care About has Borderline Personality Disorder.* Oakland, CA: New Harbinger, 2010.

Mondimore, Francis M. *Bipolar Disorder: A Guide for Patients and Families.* Baltimore: Johns Hopkins University Press, 1999.

Morrow, Jena, *Hope for the Hollow: A Thirty-Day Inside-Out Make-over for Women Recovering from Eating Disorders.* Raleigh, NC: Lighthouse Publishing, 2013.

Mueser, Kim T., and Susan Gingerich. *The Complete Family Guide to Schizophrenia: Helping Your Loved One Get the Most out of Life.* New York: Guilford Press, 2006.

Walsh, Sheila. *Loved Back to Life: How I Found the Courage to Live Free.* Nashville: Thomas Nelson, 2015.

Zayfert, Claudia, and Jason C. DeViva. *When Someone You Love Suffers from Posttraumatic Stress: What to Expect and What You can Do.* New York: Guilford Press, 2011.

Websites

Bring Change 2 Mind, www.bringchange2mind.org.

International Bipolar Foundation (IBPF), http://ibpf.org.

National Alliance on Mental Illness (NAMI), www.nami.org.

To find a counselor: www.findchristiancounselor.com or www.psychologytoday.com

Self-Injury (Self-Harm, Self-Mutilation)

Alcorn, Nancy. *Cut.* Enumclaw, WA: Winepress, 2007.

Leatham, Victoria. *Blood Letting: A Memoir of Secrets, Self-Harm, and Survival.* Oakland, CA: New Harbinger, 2006.

Strong, Marilee. *A Bright Red Scream: Self-Mutilation and the Language of Pain.* New York: Viking, 1998.

S.A.F.E. Alternatives (Self Abuse Finally Ends), selfinjury.com; Need help? Call 800-DONTCUT (366-8288) Information line.

Websites

The Butterfly Project, www.butterfly-project.tumblr.com.

Mercy Multiplied, http://mercymultiplied.com.

SAFE Alternatives (Self Abuse Finally Ends), www.selfinjury.com; information hotline: 800-DONTCUT (366-8288).

Self-Mutilators Anonymous (SMA), www.selfmutilatorsanonymous.org.

Same-Sex Attraction

Dallas, Joe. *The Gay Gospel? How Pro-Gay Advocates Misread the Bible.* Eugene, OR: Harvest House, 2007.

_____. *When Homosexuality Hits Home: What to Do When a Loved One Says They're Gay.* Eugene, OR: Harvest House, 2004.

Haley, Mike. *101 Frequently Asked Questions About Homosexuality.* Eugene, OR: Harvest House, 2004.

Johnson, Barbara. *When Your Child Breaks Your Heart: Help for Hurting Moms.* Grand Rapids: Baker Publishing, 1979.

Kaltenbach, Caleb. *Messy Grace: How a Pastor with Gay Parents Learned to Love Others Without Sacrificing Conviction.* Colorado Springs: WaterBrook, 2015.

Martin, Andrew. *Love Is an Orientation: Elevating the Conversation with the Gay Community.* Downers Grove, IL: InterVarsity, 2009.

Worthen, Anita and Bob Davies. *Someone I Love is Gay: How Family and Friends Can Respond.* Downers Grove, IL: InterVarsity, 1996.

Yuan, Christopher and Angela Yuan. *Out of a Far Country.* Colorado Springs: WaterBrook, 2011.

Websites

Lead Them Home, www.leadthemhome.org

Living Stones Ministries, www.livingstonesministries.org

Sensory Processing Disorder

Heller, Sharon. *Too Loud, Too Bright, Too Fast, Too Tight: What to Do If You Are Sensory Defensive in an Overstimulating World.* New York: Harper Collins, 2002. See also author's website: www.sharonheller.net.

Kranowitz, Carol. *The Out of Sync Child: Recognizing and Coping with Sensory Processing Disorder.* New York: Penguin, 2005. See also the STAR Center: Sensory Therapies and Research website: www.spdstar.org.

Sexual Abuse

The Healing Tree. Orange County, FL. http://caccentral.com/the-healing-tree. Search online for sexual assault programs in your county or city to find help for yourself or your child.

Heitritter, Lynn and Jeanette Vough. *Helping Victims of Sexual Abuse.* Minneapolis: Baker, 2006.

Mann, Mary Ellen. *From Pain to Power: Overcoming Sexual Trauma and Reclaiming Your True Identity.* Colorado Springs: WaterBrook, 2015.

Oakley, Diana. *Intended Harm.* Orlando, FL: Legacy Publishing, 2012.

O'Branyll, Fiona. *A Bright New Place: Triumph After Trauma.* Bloomington, IN: Westbow, 2013.

Omartian, Stormie. *Just Enough Light for the Step I'm On.* Eugene, OR: Harvest House, 2008.

Restoring the Heart Ministries (www.rthm.cc). See *In The Wildflowers*, book and support material written by Julie Woodley, a ten-part DVD series focused on recovery from sexual trauma. It was produced in cooperation with the American Association of Christian Counselors (www.aacc.net). Call 1-800-526-8673 for more information.

Victim Service Centers: Search online to find one in your county or for sexual assault hotlines.

Suicide

Biebel, David B., and Suzanne L. Foster. *Finding Your Way after the Suicide of Someone You Love.* Grand Rapids: Zondervan, 2005.

Fine, Carla. *No Time to Say Goodbye: Surviving the Suicide of a Loved One.* New York: Doubleday, 1997.

Hsu, Albert. *Grieving a Suicide: A Loved One's Search for Comfort, Answers, and Hope.* Downers Grove, IL: InterVarsity, 2002.

Jamison, Kay Redfield. *Night Falls Fast: Understanding Suicide.* New York: Knopf, 1999.

Smolin, Ann, and John Guinan, John. *Healing After the Suicide of a Loved One.* New York: Simon & Schuster, 1993.

Websites and Hotlines:

National Suicide Prevention Lifeline 1-800-273-8255 (TALK). Call 24/7 365 days a year, including holidays, www.suicidepreventionlifeline.org.

American Foundation of Suicide Prevention, www.afsp.org.

QPR Institute, www.qprinstitute.com. Offers suicide prevention training and a free e-book, *Suicide: The Forever Decision.*

The Hope Line 1-800-394-4673 (HOPE). Hope Coaches are available 24/7, www.thehopeline.com.

Hope for the Heart 1-800-4673 (HOPE). Hope Care Representatives offer real answers for real people, www.hopefortheheart.org.

Survivors of Suicide, www.survivorsofsuicide.com. Offers links to help find support groups.

To Write Love on Her Arms, www.twloha.com, A non-profit movement dedicated to presenting hope and finding help for people struggling with depression, addiction, self-injury, and suicide.

Made in the USA
Coppell, TX
17 May 2022

77879884R00105